Advance Praise for
Good Grammar is the Life of the Party

Honeycutt's approach to grammar is hilarious and refreshing. Everyone can improve their grammar by reading this book. Not only is this book funny and instructive, but readers will be surprised to find how good grammar can help you improve all areas of your life.

—*Cathy Heller, host of Don't Keep Your Day Job podcast*

Don't be fooled by the light-hearted and sometimes flat-out funny tone of this book. It's full of valuable information and tips that will serve you well in your writing.

—*Kwei Quartey, author of The Missing American*

Good Grammar is the Life of the Party is destined to be a twenty-first century classic for both rookie writers and those more experienced.

—*Dave Lieber, The Dallas Morning News*

Never before has good grammar usage been so entertaining and easy to remember. Honeycutt's humorous approach teaches correct grammar, and all writers can benefit.

—*Suzette Martinez Standring*
  Executive Director, National Society of Newspaper Columnists

There are grammar nerds and then there is Curtis Honeycutt, whose hilarious columns entertain our newspaper readers each Saturday. Now, with *Good Grammar is the Life of the Party*, they no longer have to wait for their fix of dangling modifiers, dangling mailmen, eggcorns and nounimals.

—*Karen Francisco, Fort Wayne Journal-Gazette*

Curtis is the real life of the party! His book is required reading for anyone thinking of writing anything beyond a grocery list. Laugh, think, and write better than ever!

—*Angela Kellogg, Clare County Cleaver*

Curtis Honeycutt's new book, *Good Grammar is the Life of the Party*, is a clever combination of sophisticated wit, fascinating facts, useful advice, and hilarious pop culture references. This book is so much fun—a must-read for anyone who loves to laugh and learn!

—*Lisa Smith Molinari, author of The Meat & Potatoes of Life*

The problem with Honeycutt's new book is once you start reading it, you don't want to stop. It's just that interesting.

—*Steve Kittey, Latrobe Bulletin*

I learned more about proper grammar reading Curtis Honeycutt's fantastic book, *Good Grammar is the Life of the Party*, than I did in reading the complete works of William Shakespeare, the Merriam-Webster dictionary, or Strunk and White's *The Elements of Style*. However, that may perhaps be due to not having actually read any of those other books...

—*John Branning, author of Keys To The Truculent Me: And Other Things That Drive Me Crazy*

I loved this book. I will love it again every time I reread it. I'm asking my kids to put it in my coffin when I go to Heaven. With my glasses. Just in case.

—*Kathy Eliscu, author of Not Even Dark Chocolate Can Fix This Mess*

Mark Twain said, "The difference between the right word and the almost-right word is the difference between the lightning and the lightning-bug." In his debut book, *Good Grammar is the Life of the Party*, Curtis Honeycutt takes Twain's homespun advice to heart in what may be the most entertaining book about grammar ever written.

—*Teri Rizvi, founder and director of the Erma Bombeck Writers' Workshop*

This book will help you remember grammar rules you can't keep straight and make you aware of grammar quirks you either didn't know or didn't know you knew—all while making you laugh the whole time.

—*Hannah Romero, The Rocket-Miner*

Good Grammar is the Life of the Party is hilariously insightful for those of us who manipulate (butcher?) the English language for a living. So rarely do learning and laughing go hand-in-hand as well as they do in the Grammar Guy's *Good Grammar* book.

—*Joe Southern, The Sealy News*

Good Grammar is the Life of the Party is required reading for anyone looking for a good time. You'll very much enjoy its self-effacing, eclectic style.

—*Chris Carosa, author of Hamburger Dreams: How Classic Crime Solving Techniques Helped Crack the Case of America's Greatest Culinary Mystery*

Honeycutt is genuinely funny, and he uses his humor to impart life lessons amid grammar rules told in ways you will be able to remember.

—*Lori Duff, author of If You Did What I Asked in the First Place*

GOOD GRAMMAR
IS THE LIFE OF THE PARTY

GOOD GRAMMAR IS THE Life of the PARTY

TIPS FOR A WILDLY SUCCESSFUL LIFE

CURTIS HONEYCUTT

The County
Publishing

Noblesville, Indiana

For information about permission to reproduce selections from this
book, contact The County Publishing
at thecountypublishing@gmail.com.

Published by The County Publishing
Noblesville, Indiana
thecountybooks.com

Portions of this work have previously appeared in newspapers.

Library of Congress Control Number: 2019917322

ISBN: 9780578560038
ISBN: 9780578560045 (ebook)

Cover design by Laurent Collective
laurentcollective.com

While the author has made every effort to provide accurate internet
addresses and other information at the time of publication,
neither the publisher nor the author assumes any responsibility for
errors or for changes that occur after publication. Further, the publisher
does not have any control over and does not assume any responsibility
for third-party websites or their content.

For my high school English teachers,
who taught me that words and ideas can (still)
change the world.

Contents

Introduction

This book will make your life better

"Grammar is the greatest joy in life, don't you find?"
—Lemony Snicket

Few books outside of religious holy texts (and the *Lord of the Rings* series) have a propensity to change the trajectories of readers' lives. This is one of those books.

As someone who was an English major for one semester, I am uniquely qualified to equip you with all the right grammar tools to make your life as awesome as you want it to be. Here's how I see it: there's enough good grammar for everyone. It's available to us all in unlimited quantities. In this way, grammar is better than oil, water, money, and even prize-winning miniature ponies. This is one of those "a rising tide lifts all ships" situations.

By elevating your grammar, you can elevate your status in life. This applies to your social life, work life, love life, and every other aspect of your life. Good grammar makes everything better.

Think about it this way: I recently did two things to make my life roughly 12% better. First of all, the faucet on my kitchen sink didn't spray well because I had unsuccessfully tinkered with it. Because of this, the water pressure from the faucet was slightly stronger than a trickle. After months of enduring this low-level misery, I ended up calling the good people at Kohler (who—for the record—didn't pay me to promote their excellent products) and requesting a new sprayer head nozzle[1]. Not only did they send me a new one, but they didn't even charge me for it. I put the new nozzle on correctly and now my faucet has the spraying capacity of a top-of-the-line fire department hose. This made my life 5% better.

My other 7% instant life improvement also involved home plumbing. I realize this makes me sound like a boring adult, but I'm okay with who I am. We've lived in our house for a little over three years now. It is a Victorian cottage-style home built in 1890. While we've replaced many things in the house that didn't work (furnaces, air conditioners, gutters, etc.), we hadn't yet replaced anything that worked on a basic level.

When we moved in, the toilets in each of our two bathrooms had matching off-colored rings stained into the porcelain of their bowls. While they were technically clean, they looked gross. Additionally, you had to flush each of the toilets a certain way—almost like a secret, lavatorial handshake—so that the water would stop running once the bowl refilled.

As this became a sustained, mild annoyance in my daily life, I decided to put a stop to it. I bought two brand new toilets from Lowe's (who also haven't given me a dime for this commercial) and brought them home. Then my friend, Bo, came over to remove the old (technically functional) toilets, install the new ones, and make the old ones disappear. As Bo loaded the old toilets into the back of his handyman truck, I felt like the kingpin of the toilet mafia. I didn't care where the old problem

---

1   Nozzle is a great word. The more I say it, the more it sounds made-up. Nozzle.

toilets went as long as I never saw them again. Our new toilets, made by the good people at Kohler, are fantastic. They have increased my quality of living by 7%. The old toilets are probably at the bottom of the White River, swimming with the fish.

Why am I telling you these stories about faucets and toilets? Sometimes we have things in our lives that, if changed, could incrementally improve our lives. Each of the short grammar lessons in this book can boost your success bar a few notches at a time. Taken as a whole, this book can turn you into a sophisticated grammar aficionado. People will stop you on the street to take selfies with you. You'll receive applause when you enter rooms. You may even have a stretch of highway named after you.

The morals of this story? First of all, invest stock in Kohler.[2] Secondly, read this book cover to cover: it will change your life.

---

2   I've been told Kohler is a privately-held company. Perhaps one day it will go public and we can get in on the ground floor of this sure thing.

Second Introduction

Put away the red pen

I like introductions like Hobbits like breakfasts, so I think I'll have another. Also, I want you to note well that you are getting page credit for reading this book's preliminary essays. You don't get credit for reading pages in other books with lower-case Roman numerals.[1] You're welcome.

Do you want to correct people's grammar or do you want to have friends?

You can either be a "grammar Nazi[2]," the "grammar police," the "grammar assistant to the regional deputy" or you can have friends. It's as simple as that.

You can't have your judgment cake and eat it, too.

Am I suggesting we let people go on willy-nilly, using the wrong "there/their/they're" or "your/you're?" Not necessarily. I'm suggesting that we don't act like grammar jerks.

---

1 I want to give a quick shout-out to my friend, 54.

2 Godwin's Law of Nazi Analogies states that "as an online discussion grows longer, the probability of a comparison involving Nazis or Hitler approaches 1." Don't be a grammar Nazi.

If you glean one lesson from reading this book, it's this: don't be a jerk. When you lord your grammar prowess over someone (especially in public), no one's going to want to hang out with you. Feel free to be right: you'll soon find yourself correcting an empty room.

Grammar plays a crucial role in our language and communication. However, to quote Uncle Ben (from Spider-Man, not the guy on the rice box), "With great power comes great responsibility."

Just because we have the nuclear codes doesn't mean we should use them to kill gnats.

In this book, when I refer to "grammar," I'm casting a wide net over the English language, specifically as it relates to American English. This will include actual grammar, punctuation, spelling, syntax and anything else that can fit under this large, linguistic umbrella. And, as I'm casting a wide net, I can't hope to cover every grammar issue that gets your goat, so to speak.

While I will discuss these grammar topics with a light-hearted tone, I hope to convince you that your life can actually prosper (at least partly) due to good grammar. I'm serious. You catch more flies with honey than with vinegar, as they say.

Social Success

How good grammar will win you friends and make you the star at any party

"You've got to fight for your right to party."
—Beastie Boys

You don't have to put on airs to get people to like you. You don't even have to have an heir. You simply need to have good grammar skills.

Do you want an entire wall of your living room to feature an aquarium that houses a variety of rare shark species? Work on your grammar.

Are you interested in being *Time*'s person of the year? Learn proper punctuation.

Do you want to have a secret room in your house devoted to rare first editions and one of those cool old library ladders on wheels? Brush up on your spelling. And while we're at it, I really think you should upgrade your château's library to the "deluxe" package; it comes with the feature everyone wants where you tilt an old copy of Chaucer's *Canterbury Tales* at a

45-degree angle and the hinges of an unseen door creak open, revealing a room full of even more books. You do have to pay an upcharge for the creaky hinges, but it's so worth it.

Yes—good grammar will make your life more awesome. It can transform you from an ugly duckling who gets picked last for the kickball team to an elegant swan who gets V.I.P. treatment from foreign dignitaries. In short, good grammar will help you climb the ranks of the social elite and the celebrity tastemakers. You'll be like Beyoncé crossed with Kate Middleton, with the charm of James Bond.

Before you become this social butterfly, you've got to get a handle on things people like, as well as key grammar concepts that will unlock the doors to your massive success. So, get ready to curl up into a grammar cocoon—soon you'll emerge a gorgeous, popular social butterfly.

○ ○ ○ ○ ○

Things People Like

Big, swanky parties

Do you want to get invited to cool parties? Get your grammar ducks in a row. The fact is, grammar is everywhere. But, as soon as someone identifies himself as an expert, you can almost always safely assume he's going to judge you any time you end a sentence with a preposition.

I'm no grammar czar; I'm just here to help improve your grammar and make your life more awesome.

Good grammar is wonderful because it opens doors: to job interviews, romantic relationships, and even elegant parties where people drink wine served from bottles (I always thought it came only in boxes). By improving your grammar, your Facebook friends will rightly assume you've started wearing a gold-rimmed monocle while playing polo on your yacht. Fancy!

Let's start with your family. Yeah, we're going there. Specifically, when you want to sign your family's collective name on a holiday card or get it laser etched on a fake rock for your front lawn, how do you write it? Is it *The Millers* or *The Miller's?*

If you get this one right, your family holiday card distribution list is sure to soar well over 1,000 friends, family and influential social acquaintances.

Everyone likes a good party (after all, that's why you're improving your grammar, right?), and apostrophes are like sentence confetti, adding a fun flair to your scintillating syntax. But a misplaced apostrophe is like confetti at a funeral: inappropriate and impossible to undo.

To make your last name plural, never add an apostrophe. Just don't do it. This is correct:

The Millers went to the KISS concert.

Adding an apostrophe to your last name makes it possessive:

Did you see The Millers' cool new van?

If your last name ends with s, z, x, ch or sh, simply add *-es* to make it plural:

Season's greetings from The Foxes.

If your last name ends in any other letter (including y), simply add an *-s*:

The Honeycutts are incredibly photogenic.

So, if you're considering adding your family's name to the back of your luxury yacht, write *The Millers*. Adding an apostrophe will simply get you uninvited from those swanky boat parties, leaving you to drink your boxed wine, alone and sad while you wistfully stalk everyone else's happy boat photos on

Facebook, Instagram, Next Door, or whatever app the cool kids are using this week.

I'm not looking to drop the grammar hammer down on anyone; no one likes that guy. Instead, I'm rooting for you to get your act together so you can do some jealousy-inducing name-dropping at your next invitation-only brunch at the country club.

○ ○ ○ ○ ○

Small, exclusive parties

It's not just about the big, swanky parties, though. Parties, galas and soirées are all about quality over quantity. As an introvert, I prefer a humble high-roller blackjack table in the back room of a casino in Monaco to a backyard bash where everyone's invited. This is especially true for me when it comes to celebrating my birthday.

In fact, I celebrated my birthday last year. This year, it will probably happen again.

Okay, maybe "celebrated" isn't quite accurate. Let's say I recently endured another birthday. And, as much as I openly dislike birthday attention, this got me thinking: how do I properly write about age and numbers?

Some say you're only as old as you act. In that case, I'm 11 years old. Just ask my three-year-old son.

Did you notice the two ways I wrote about ages just now? Both instances are correct.

Here's the rule: only add hyphens when the age is used as an adjective that comes before the noun you are modifying. For example:

> We haven't been getting any sleep thanks to our three-month-old daughter.

In this case, the adjective (three-month-old) comes before

the noun (daughter) it describes.

If the noun comes before the age, don't use a hyphen. For example:

> Curtis is 33 years old.

In this case, the rapidly aging noun (Curtis) is 33, the same number as Larry Bird's jersey.

So, when do you write out a number and when do you simply use a numeral? As a general rule, spell out numbers one through nine and use numerals for numbers 10 and larger. Many style guides disagree, because if they all had the same rules, we'd only need one book. Of course, there are exceptions to this numerical rule, such as when you want to have consistency in your sentence. For example:

> At the time of this book's printing, Curtis owns 1 airplane (which is made out of paper), while Lufthansa owns 401 (which are probably made out of metal).

In this case, it would look strange to write out "one" and then use a numeral (401), so I used numerals for both.

Whether you write it with letters or numerals, age is merely a number. In this roundabout we call life, we all get off at our own exits, because otherwise we'd all be dizzy. Relational ties are the hyphens that bind us together with the people we love. As long as I can have a low-key birthday with a handful of my favorite people, I'm happy; just don't have the waiters at the restaurant shove a tortilla chip sombrero with a guacamole moat on my head and cause a big scene.

If you play your numbers right, you can beat the house and impress your tuxedo and evening gown-clad jet-setters. Just don't tell them it's your birthday.

○ ○ ○ ○ ○

Private helicopters & private islands

Here's something that impresses the cufflinks off well-to-do socialites: private things. I don't mean to say "unmentionable" private things (keep those to yourself, please). I mean private things like helicopters and islands.

And when we invite people to spend a long weekend at our private islands, we don't want to sound dumb. For that reason we need to get *who* and *whom* straightened out.

Every time I'm tempted to use whom, I'm afraid of sounding like I own a fancy, private helicopter to travel to my private island where I roll around in gold coins, Scrooge McDuck-style. It just kind of sounds snooty. So let's learn how to use it correctly, shall we?

I have an easy way to remember when to use who or whom: Use who when you can replace it in a sentence with he; use *whom* when you can replace it in a sentence with *him*. For example:

> Who/Whom tried to parachute out of my private helicopter? Bad idea, dude.

Let's try replacing *who/whom* with *him*:

> Him tried to parachute out of my private helicopter. Bad idea, dude.

That doesn't sound right. How about *he*:

> He tried to parachute out of my private helicopter. Bad idea, dude.

That sounds better, so we should use *who* in this sentence. Another example:

> Who/Whom did you invite over to your secret island

bungalow this weekend?

Which sounds right:

I invited he over to my secret island bungalow this weekend

-or-

I invited him to my secret island bungalow this weekend.

Him sounds better, so we should use *whom* in this example. He/him is simply a secret, tricky way to determine the subject and object of a sentence. The subject is the person (or place or thing) doing the action in a sentence. The object is the person (or place or thing) on the receiving end of the action.

To whom (object) did Gary (subject) direct his cheesy pick-up lines?

Since we usually don't think in terms of subject and object, I think it's simpler to use the *he/him* trick.

In my opinion, going around using whom properly probably makes people assume you have an entire closet just for your polo ascots, but I always enjoy a rollicking, post-brunch polo match on the beach of my exclusive pretend island.

Do you want to know the easiest way to become the owner of your personal private island?

Step 1: Design a flag with your personal logo on it.
Step 2: Get the flag printed and installed on a flag pole.
Step 3: Find an island you'd like to have.
Step 4: Plant your flag on the beach of the island.
Step 5: You own it (See article 19 of the Magna Carta, also known as the "make it, take it" or "finders keepers" clause).

This approach has worked with few (if any) historically negative consequences. Now you just have to survey a suitably flat area for your helipad.

○ ○ ○ ○ ○

Country club etiquette

I've never belonged to a country club, but I once helped a friend photograph a large event at a prominent country club in Indianapolis. Can you believe the price tag to join is $30,000?

There's a waiting list to get in.

In the country club world, they probably hear this one all the time:

> I feel badly because Randolph lost his job at the pro shop.

In an effort to use better grammar we can often make our grammar worse. Let's figure out why the correct phrase in the above instance should be "I feel bad."

The key here is knowing the difference between action verbs and linking verbs. The correct way to identify an action verb seems rather obvious: it does something active. Active verbs like *gobble, decide, shimmy, impeach* and *frolic* tell us the action being performed in a sentence. Linking verbs, on the other hand, connect the subject of a sentence to information about that subject.

Linking verbs do not describe an action. Therefore, use adverbs to describe action verbs and adjectives to describe linking verbs.

Sensory-related verbs like *feel, look, smell, taste* and *sound* can either be used as linking verbs or active verbs, depending on the context of the sentence. Kind of confusing, if you ask me.

In our example where poor Randy got the heave-ho from

the pro shop, *feel* is used as a linking verb. *I feel bad* describes the state of my emotions because Randolph was let go. The only way *I feel badly* is correct is if, after being fired, Randolph got in his souped-up golf cart, put the pedal to the metal and—in an act of blind rage—he ran over all ten of my fingers as I carefully attempted to replace one of my several divots, rendering my sense of touch useless. In this case, "I feel badly because Randolph lost his job at the pro shop" would be correct.

With sensory verbs, it's important to identify whether the verb is an active verb or a linking verb. The way I always remember this takes me back to my tremendous AP English teacher, Dr. Ballard, who used this example: Only Captain Hook feels badly. Get it? Because he has a hook for a hand.

Would Captain Hook make a good masseuse? No, because Captain Hook feels badly. And he probably feels pretty bad about that. And I'm not sure he could get a job at the pro shop even if he wanted to; I'm sure his background check would come back suspect. Plus, when it comes to your golf game, hooking and slicing are frowned upon.

What in the word?

An *isle* is an island.
An *aisle* is a narrow walkway.
I'll is a contraction for *I will*.

It's all good

According to G.K. Chesterton, "The word 'good' has many meanings. For example, if a man were to shoot his grandmother at a range of five hundred yards, I should call him a good shot, but not necessarily a good man." First of all, I have to tip my cap to Chesterton's excellent use of the subjunctive case when he uses *were* in the second sentence. Secondly, *well* and *good* are often misunderstood in our language.

"I know the difference between well and good," your inner voice is probably yelling right now. Great—you get a gold star! Let's review, shall we? *Good* is an adjective while *well* is an adverb (most of the time). We'll get to the "most of the time" part in a second.

Here's what you already know about *good* and *well*. *Good* is an adjective. It should always be used to describe or modify nouns. For example:

Nate is a good sportswriter.

Well is (almost) always an adverb. Use it to modify a verb, adverb or an adjective. For example:

He writes about the Chiefs well.

He does his job well.

Now it's time to reconcile the confusing exceptions. Only use *well* as an adverb when using linking verbs (including *be, look,* or *feel*) that describe the state of someone's health.

Monica wasn't feeling well the time her hand got chopped off.

Yesterday I was sick; today I am well.

I don't feel well because I drank some water from the dilapidated well.

If we use *well* to describe someone's health, we use *good* to describe someone's emotional state of being.

LeBron felt good about his decision to take his talents to Miami.

Byron didn't feel good after he lied to his kids about Santa.

In these cases, we're using *good* as an adverb. Did you ever know it was okay to use *good* as an adverb? My mind is blown.

So, the next time someone asks you how you're doing, you can say "I'm doing good" or "I'm doing well." Depending on how you choose to answer the question, it's perfectly acceptable to say *well* or *good*, although, I suspect if your hand gets chopped off, you probably don't feel very well or very good.

○ ○ ○ ○ ○

Staying on top of hot vegetable trends

One thing that really impresses people is fancy vegetable-cutting techniques. To score big points at ritzy after-brunch parties, show off your mad cutting board skills. You can chop, mince, dice, slice, julienne, brunoise and chiffonade your way into thinking you're some kind of Michelin-star chef. And, while you're at it, stay up on the latest veggie fads.

A few years ago, kale was all the rage at the local farmers market. After that we were hit with a massive avocado fad which elevated toast prices among the millennial hipster community. As a professional grammarian and amateur vegetable trend forecaster, I urge you to take this hot tip: you're going to want to put all your stock in the next big thing to hit the farm-to-table craze: Brussels sprouts.

Before you object to this up-and-coming veggie trend based on how your mom used to make Brussels sprouts (boiled beyond oblivion), I'm told there are now more interesting and tasty ways to prepare these cute little cabbages (roasted with sea salt and olive oil, for one).

And it's spelled *Brussels sprouts,* not *brussel sprouts.* You could theoretically have one Brussels sprout, I suppose. Even though they originated in the Mediterranean region, Brussels sprouts gained popularity across Europe, especially in Belgium, where they received their geographical moniker. And— yes—I capitalized the *B* in Brussels sprouts.

For that matter, what about the *F* in French toast? French fries certainly don't always get the capital treatment. In the United Nations of foods, there's not much capitalization consistency. Will the delegation from Switzerland be offended if Swiss cheese isn't capitalized?

One argument against capitalizing any noun phrase containing a place word is that you should call Brussels sprouts *Brussels sprouts* with a capital *B* if (and only if) they did, indeed, originate from the city of Brussels. If they didn't actually hail from the geographical region, argues the Chicago Manual of Style, you don't need to capitalize them.

I'm going to have to disagree with the "never capitalize" camp. I've never seen baked Alaska with a lowercase *a,* even though the flambéed dessert most likely wasn't sourced and shipped from our 49th state. The same rule applies to Swiss chard, Dijon mustard, Gorgonzola cheese, Canadian bacon and the Cuban sandwich.

I guess that makes me an all-or-nothing capitalizer; so be it. Either capitalize proper nouns contained in common phrases or don't. Just because your Hawaiian pizza wasn't made in Hawaii (the pineapple and ham pizza monstrosity actually originated in Canada, of all places) doesn't mean you demote Hawaii to a common noun with a lowercase *h.*

One thing I can guarantee is that Brussels sprouts are the new kale; so if you pride yourself as the first among your friends to find the latest veggie trends, jump on the bandwagon before it gets too crowded. If you serve Brussels sprouts next to your cheese plate at your next party, you can bet you'll get invited to the next big event.

Fancy roof parties

I know this guy whose goal in college was to stand on the roof of every building on his campus. Sure, his priority should have been to get good grades, but I respected his ambition. Although pretty much every building has a roof, roofs themselves are exclusive. You can't just take the elevator to the roof; you have to either know the right person, have a really tall ladder or be a bird.

I hope somebody invites me to a party on a roof someday. To achieve this not-quite-bucket-list dream of mine would make me feel as if I had finally achieved a (literally) high social status. I can picture myself swirling a martini, talking about racehorses and stocks with some guy wearing a monocle; it would be so luxurious...

...unless, of course, that roof party happened on a sloped roof. Inevitably someone (probably Karl, the mailman) would slip, and I'd have to burst into action, interrupting a perfectly pleasant conversation about dressage to catch poor Karl as he dangled precariously from the edge of the roof. The lesson here? Make sure your party roof is a flat one before you book the venue.

Dangling modifiers are equally as scary as dangling mailmen. To understand what a dangling modifier is (and why we should avoid them), let's start with understanding modifiers. A modifier is a word or phrase that adds description to another word or phrase. When modifiers are used correctly, you'll find them right next to the words they're describing.

When you see a dangling modifier lurking in a sentence, the sentence will be confusing. Dangling modifiers often show up at the beginning or end of a sentence:

> After spending a week on the solar panel, Mabel unsuccessfully tried to eat the melted chocolate bar.

Due to the placement of the first clause, you'd think Mabel

had been on the solar panel all week.

> When in kindergarten, my mom drove us to school.

This sentence implies my mom was a kindergartner when she drove us to school. That can't be right!

Because of these awkward sentence structures, the modifiers change the meaning from the sentences' intentions. Allow me to correct the sentences so we can all feel better about life.

> Mabel unsuccessfully tried to eat the melted chocolate bar after it had spent a week on the solar panel.

> When I was in kindergarten, my mom drove us to school.

So, just as you need to make sure your roof party is happening on a flat roof, you should take care to place your modifiers right next to (before or after) the word or phrase they modify. Doing so will avoid sentence catastrophes (as well as keep our buddy Karl alive). Don't leave Karl or your modifiers hanging.

○ ○ ○ ○ ○

How to pick out the best chandelier for your foyer

A preposition is a terrible thing to end a sentence with.
—*Winston S. Churchill*

My goal isn't to be super rich. I don't think I'll ever be afflicted with wealth, but if I end up wealthy as a result of selling millions of books or being the cover model for a hat catalog for people with big heads, I know exactly which catalog I'd like to get. In the unlikely event that my bank account grows by a multiple tens of thousands of dollars, I want to order one of everything from the Neiman Marcus Christmas Catalog. I'd buy a solar-powered yacht, a crystal rhinoceros statue, an Italian leather hot dog couch and a 2022 first-round pick. Is there anything we can't order from a fancy catalog?

The people who lived in our house before us had some really good tastes in catalogs. Instead of canceling them, we started ordering stuff from these catalogs (which included the actual J. Peterman catalog). Even two years later, we still get mail items addressed to these intriguing former residents. In fact, one of them has some serious business to do with the I.R.S. I suppose that's better than having serious business to do with I.B.S.

If your goal in life is to spend your weekends perusing chandelier catalogs while wearing a gold-rimmed monocle in one of your five lake châteaus, you probably should brush up on your grammar. Now we're going to focus on ending sentences with prepositions, which is almost universally seen as a big no-no by traditional grammar aficionados.

Before I surprise you with my take on the subject, let's revisit what prepositions are in the first place. A preposition is a word that connects a noun to another nearby word or phrase in a sentence. I know—that's confusing. Let me give you some examples:

> The new chandelier hung (over) the ballroom.

> Joe showed off his basic box step skills (during) the waltz portion of the gala.

> The valet locked my keys (inside) my Lamborghini again.

Supposedly it's a huge grammar faux pas to end a sentence with a preposition. In most cases, I agree. Here's the number one case in which you shouldn't end a sentence with a preposition: when the preposition is unnecessary.

Here's an example:

Where did you put your keys at?

The reason this sentence is wrong is that *at* is unnecessary. If it read: "Where did you put your keys?" the meaning would stay the same.

Here's where some old-school grammarians will wag their fingers at me: when you have to drastically and unnaturally alter your sentence structure to avoid ending a sentence with a preposition, don't worry about it. By doing so, you either sound way too formal or like you're doing a Yoda impression. Instead of saying "The polo match was rained out," people will contort their sentence into, "Rained out the polo match was." When I read that, my inner narrator sounds precisely like Luke Skywalker's tiny green guru.

Sure, it's important to maintain formal sentence structure when the occasion calls for it: in a job cover letter, in academic papers and when ordering at multi-Michelin star restaurants. But, in everyday usage, ending the occasional sentence in a preposition isn't a big deal. If dramatically altering your sentences to avoid ending them in prepositions makes them sound super awkward and overly formal, you may just need to lighten up.

I'm sure you were wondering: what's the sign of a good chandelier? You can't tell a good chandelier the same way you can tell if a watermelon's ripe. Thumping a chandelier is frowned upon in the luxury lighting section of Pottery Barn. You can tell a quality chandelier based on the authenticity of its crystals. To verify, consult a wandering fortune teller in the nearest foggy meadow. Her name is Janet. Tell her I sent you.

What in the word?

To *ensure* is to make sure something happens.
To *insure* is to cover something with an insurance policy.
To *assure* is to take away someone's doubts.

A guy who knows his wines

There are two types of people in this world: *whiners* and *winers*.
Whiners complain when things don't go their way. Winers find
a sophisticated-sounding excuse to get drunk. You have to pick
your poison, I suppose.

And, while we're on the subject of wine, have you had a
canned wine yet? It's exactly what it sounds like: wine from a
can. Don't snicker; the quality of canned wine has increased
steadily over the past several years. It's portable and potable.
What's not to like? I'm fine with it, and canned wine continues
to get finer itself.

When it comes to the finer things in life, some people have
distinctly refined tastes. They can tell the difference between a
St. Francis and a Sterling Cabernet Sauvignon. And—yes—I did
just ask Google about high-end, expensive red wines in order
to make that comparison. Others couldn't tell one of Napa Valley's
best bottles of wine from a box of Franzia. In their opinions,
both wines "get the job done," so to speak.

Let's look at one of grammar's narrow distinctions: when to
use *different than* and when to use *different from*. So, grab your
grammar ascots, because it's about to get fancy up in here.

In general, *different from* is the preferred phrase among
grammar aficionados. It's an adjective phrase that is used to
compare two things. Here are a few examples:

> Marty proved that he was different from the rest of the
> presidential debate field with his impromptu flute solo.

> Although the new *Space Wars* movies had special effects
> different from the originals, I think they're all pretty
> much the same movie.

Although *different than* shouldn't be employed as often,
it does have its merits. Like *different from*, *different than* is an
adjective phrase used to compare two things. What makes it

unique is that the phrase often gets divided. For example:

> Nate selected a different Fabergé egg than the one Noah picked.

> I understood Barry's new neck tattoo to represent something much different than your interpretation.

> Mike took a different route than I did to get to the monster truck rally.

Different from is seen as the gold standard among editors, linguists and grammarians, although some people can't really notice a difference (as in our wine example). In general, use *different from*. An easy way to remember this is that *from* starts with *f*, just like *formal* does. So, in any formal writing, make sure you use *different from;* the grammar enthusiasts will think you're one of them.

Can the Nobel committee hand out awards for impeccable grammar? Just because they haven't doesn't mean they won't. Keep it up and your chances of NEGOT-ing will increase every day.

○ ○ ○ ○ ○

Saying the right thing at a party

> *"Which is him?" The grammar was faulty, maybe, but we could not know, then, that it would go in a book someday.*
> — *Mark Twain, Roughing It*

There's an old adage that advises against talking about the following three subjects at a social gathering: money, religion and politics. I'd like to add to that list. Stay away from mentioning any strange rashes, avoid bringing up your fondness for sniffing gasoline fumes and leave out the anecdote about the day you forgot to wear pants to the grocery store.

As our cultural considerations become more accepting over time, we also need to be mindful of how we address people. Our cultural understanding of LGBTQ rights has progressed considerably, but we've still got a long way to go (which is akin to saying hammerhead sharks have more to learn about the rules of the road before they'll be issued driver's licenses).

And, while we should collectively seek to understand the non-binary nuances of gender and sexuality, grammar has stepped in to provide some clarity (thanks, grammar). For instance, the AP Stylebook recently made a significant rule change, adding *they* as an acceptable singular pronoun. According to the AP, "They/them/their is acceptable in limited cases as a singular and-or gender-neutral pronoun, when alternative wording is overly awkward or clumsy. However, rewording usually is possible and always is preferable."

Up until now, I've been against using *they* as an acceptable singular pronoun, as it's often used as a grammar mistake. Take, for example, Fergie's 2006 hit "Big Girls Don't Cry" in which the artist sings "And I'm gonna miss you like a child misses their blanket." Every time I heard this song on the radio, I'd judge Fergie (or whoever wrote the song) for his/her/their incorrect pronoun usage. I suppose I expected the newly solo Black Eyed Pea to incorporate better grammar into her lyrics. Either way, I like making the *they/them/their* exception when it comes to issues of gender inclusivity.

According to the AP, clarity is key here, primarily because the word *they* has always served strictly as a plural pronoun, or so I thought. Apparently using the singular *they* as a non-binary pronoun has been in use since the thirteenth century. Over the years, writers including Shakespeare, Dickens, Austen, and Shaw have used *they* as a singular pronoun.

But as newer, experimental gender-neutral pronouns including *xe* and *ze* haven't yet gained popular adoption or garnered widespread awareness, *they* is acceptable, as long as it's clear to whom the writer is referring. When possible, GLAAD points out, it makes sense to use the subject's name for clarity purposes, although that can quickly become redundant.

Just as we need to develop a better understanding of gender-inclusive pronouns, we need to make sure we're becoming increasingly pro-people. I know issues of gender and sexuality are delicate subjects. However, as culture and language drive each other forward, rules change. Usage shifts. People gain understanding. And, regardless of what gender a person identifies as, everyone deserves to be treated with dignity and respect: these are our inalienable rights.

This conversation is becoming increasingly less theoretical and more personal as more people summon the courage to challenge gender norms and, more importantly, embrace their authentic selves. Since grammar and gender have collided into the same topic, I thought I'd bring it up for us to consider thoughtfully. If it gets me uninvited from your next party, then so be it.

○ ○ ○ ○ ○

A party trick that will knock their socks off

I don't want to tell you how to live your life, but I think the more jobs you have and the more adventurous trips you take while you're young will expand your horizons and will help you to understand people better. Not only that, but you'll have cool stories to tell at parties and you'll know which foods give you bouts of I.B.S.[1] I forget: was that one of the things we're not supposed to talk about?

Everyone's on the lookout for their next clever party anecdote for that awkward pause between the cheese course and the *amuse-bouche* (I know I am). The perfect quip at exactly the right time will make you feel like a million bucks in the tuxedo that people are now assuming you own. If you memorize this

---

1   Wow, the second I.B.S. reference already. This definitely merits its own index listing.

next grammar gem, you're guaranteed to be the hero at the next soirée or gala you attend.

Do you remember the mnemonic device from math that goes "Please excuse my dear Aunt Sally"? This helps you remember the order of operations in a math equation (parentheses, exponents, multiplication, division, addition, subtraction). In English, there's an equivalent, but largely unknown "order of operations" for the order in which adjectives go in front of a noun. Even more shocking is that this rule is taught to most non-native speakers, but native speakers are never taught it.

The order is:
- Quantity
- Opinion
- Size
- Physical Quality
- Shape
- Age
- Color
- Origin
- Material
- Type
- Purpose
- Noun

We are never formally taught this adjective order, but we know that "five wrinkly octogenarian bronze Italian sunbathers" sounds correct (albeit an odd scenario), but if you say "octogenarian five Italian wrinkly bronze sunbathers," you sound like a total weirdo. You don't know how you know that's wrong; you just know it.

Let's try it with some simpler phrases. You'd never say *old little lady*; you would always say *little old lady*. Likewise, *blue suede shoes* sounds right, but you would never say *suede blue shoes*. You've probably heard someone remark about their baby's *big brown eyes*, but if that same parent went on about their baby's *brown big eyes* you'd think something was wrong with them. Try saying these phrases out loud and you'll hear how truly ridiculous adjectives in the wrong order sound to your English-preferring ears.

And, while I don't have a clever mnemonic device for adjective order, it's something you should feel privileged not to know—unless, that is, you want to be the talk of your town's small secretive Sicilian social circle.

○ ○ ○ ○ ○

Sweet yacht, bro

I've never been fond of boats or horses. The reason I'm not a boat fan is that I'm a 33-year-old man who can't swim. And I don't want to get into the horse thing right now. I'm still working through that with my counselor. Let's just say it happened back in 2009 on a rainy spring day in Arizona and I don't want to talk about it. The horse's name was Azul. I almost died. That's all you're getting out of me.

At some point during summertime childhood swimming lessons, I failed miserably and didn't receive my certificate to move to the next swim class. As a result, I dropped out. For a pasty redhead, I already didn't like being outside in the first place. Now I can barely doggie paddle my way out of a kiddie pool.

If I were hypothetically to win a sailboat or modest yacht, I'd certainly sell it as quickly as possible. I'd put that sail up for sale. The difference between the words sail, sale, sell and cell are salient. And, before you can accuse me of being a sellout, let me assure you, as does the theoretical starter yacht, this argument will hold water.

First, let's tackle the difference between *sail* and *sale*. *Sail* can be used as both a noun and a verb. As a noun, *sail* refers to a piece of fabric attached to a boat to help power it using wind. As a verb, *sail* refers to a trip taken on a sailboat.

Most of what I know about sailboats I learned from The Beach Boys' version of "Sloop John B."

A *sale* is a noun that refers to the act of selling, specifically when a good or service is traded for some kind of currency. For example:

> Mattress stores all think it's a great idea to have big sales over Labor Day weekend. It's as if the store owners all got together and decided to celebrate hard work by giving people a great excuse to do the exact opposite.

Sale is different from *sell*, which is a verb; it is the act of working towards the goal of making the sale. You can sell a boat. Once you sell the boat, you have made a sale.

A *cell* is a noun. It can refer to a few different things. A cell is a small room in which a prisoner is locked. A cell is also a small group acting within a larger organization. A cell is a basic structural unit of all organisms. A cell is a battery. *Cell* is short for *cellular*, so some people refer to their cellular or mobile phones as their *cell* or, more commonly, *cell phone*.

I hope my clarification of *sail, sale, sell* and *cell* went swimmingly—which is more than I can say about my own swimming skills. I do plan to take one-on-one adult swimming lessons at some point; it's not exactly "cool" to show up to a friend's hot tub cocktail party wearing a lifejacket over one's swim shirt.

What in the word?

Already is when something has happened in the past.
All ready is when someone is prepared for something.

Horses with clever names

This is the sort of arrant pedantry up with which I will not put.
—Winston S. Churchill

I said I didn't want to get into it, but here I am, getting into it. My wife, Carrie, and I went to Arizona one year to catch some Cubs spring training games. We were there the only week all season that it was cool and rainy. We did get to meet hall-of-fame pitcher Rollie Fingers and his exquisitely twisty mustache, but other than that, the trip was a wash, literally and figuratively speaking.

For the purposes of your inner narrator, feel free to queue up the song "A Horse with No Name" by America on YouTube or on your turntable.

Carrie and I decided to try horseback riding during a break in the weather one day. Before we were introduced to our steeds, Carrie and I had to sign an injury waiver which stated that if the horses killed us, it was our own dumb faults.

After Carrie and I signed our death wishes, the horse instructor person led us to the helmet area. Carrie found a helmet that fit her appropriately-proportioned head; I, on the other hand, am a human bobblehead doll. The horse riding facility didn't have a helmet big enough for my giant melon (I wear a 7 ¾ size fitted hat). The instructor was quick to point out that I had already signed the waiver; if I cracked my skull, I'd have to foot my own hospital bill.

Our instructor introduced Carrie and me to our horses. Carrie's was named something cheeky like Harry Trotter or Hermioneigh—I can't quite remember. I got paired with Azul, a menacing horse who appeared to be sizing me up from across the pasture. The beast stared at me with his beady little soulless black eyes while he chewed some kind of stringy-looking grass. With a low-pitched grunt, Azul emitted puffs of smoke from his fiery demon horse nostrils as he dared me to climb on his back.

As I hurled my leg over the side of the horse, Azul broke into a brisk gallop. I tried to pull on his reins, but that only emboldened the demon steed. "Sir, the horse can sense your fear!" the instructor offered. Thanks, lady.

All the instructor could offer was her useless refrain: "Pull back hard, he can sense your fear." Without a helmet, I clung to the very creature that now threatened my life. Azul, at a full sprint, turned around on a dime, flinging me around violently as he ran perilously close to various forms of onlooking cacti. I hung on.

Soon I realized Azul was ticked at me because I had interrupted him during his midday grass snack. I can't prove it, but I think my horse was chewing on the neighbor's marijuana crop. It was time for me to get off this high horse.

In fact, I think we all need to get off our high horses.

We've probably all written a version of the same last-minute essay at some point in high school or college: you've read the assigned book (okay, *skimmed* is probably more accurate) and there's a five-page essay due tomorrow. Well, technically it's due today because it's 2:00 a.m. and your paper's due at 9:00. It's time to *fill the space*, as they say in university circles. You've nudged the margins to make them bigger. You're using Courier New because it takes up more space on the page. Now it's time to make your words longer and more intelligent-sounding so you can squeak out a B-minus on this bad boy. You consult your thesaurus for every third word.

Somehow we learn a certain form of writing an essay or paper that ends up resembling everyone else's papers, or—even worse— an imitation of our professor's speech patterns. The result is a flowery, academic-sounding, five-page whopper of a nothingburger. You swap out the word *use* for *utilize* or *employ*. You go to great lengths in order to avoid ending a sentence with a preposition, forcing your words to twist and turn into stuffy syntax riddles. You're verbose to the point of long-windedness.

There's a term for this: Engfish. It's when we use contrived language for the sake of sounding smart. We use Engfish in our writing and in conversations. By puffing up our discourse we end up obscuring our intended message.

In a 1946 article entitled "Politics and the English Language," George Orwell suggested six rules for combating our tendency to write in this way:

1. Never use a metaphor, simile or other figure of speech which you are used to seeing in print.
2. Never use a long word where a short one will do.
3. If it is possible to cut a word out, always cut it out.
4. Never use the passive where you can use the active.
5. Never use a foreign phrase, a scientific word or a jargon word if you can think of an everyday English equivalent.
6. Break any of these rules sooner than say anything outright barbarous.

I'm with Orwell on this one. It's not bad to sound smart; I'm suggesting the best way to communicate is by putting your thesaurus away and saying what you mean to say. Don't sugarcoat it; don't even coat it at all. Just give them the naked, unvarnished truth. Do this and your communication will be strong and effective.

○ ○ ○ ○ ○

Fancy foyer art

When guests arrive for your wine-swishing soirée, you're going to want to have a piece of art hanging in your foyer that really punches them in the teeth. You need some art that says, "Man, now that is some art!" The piece needs to be bigger than a van, and it should be surrounded by a thick, gold-leafed frame that screams *expensive*.

In real life, I work at an arts nonprofit, and I see all kinds of art on a daily basis. Some of it is marvelous, and some of it is just *meh*. Art quality really is subjective. Some paintings look as if you'd buy them at a TJ Maxx or Homegoods store and hang in your bathroom. There's nothing wrong with that. Even though I don't have a background in fine art, I now know what a palette knife is. I really like a good alley mural, whether it was legally sanctioned by the building owners or not. I appreciate art that is out in the open, available for anyone to see.

I'll admit it: I don't know much about street art. I'm no graffitist (a person who does graffiti), but I do know that to "tag" something is when someone quickly spray paints a surface, or it can indicate the way a graffiti artist signs his/her work. I'm aware that I'm breaking down basic graffiti terms mostly to win points with the Gen Z crowd. You can take that one to the Banksy![2]

I appreciate clothing companies that have stopped adding tags to their shirts. Instead of adding the tag, they print the size and washing instructions directly on the inside of the shirt. Just like that: no more back of the neck irritation! I'm glad someone finally figured that out. If there's a sartorial equivalent of the Nobel prize, we should track down the inventor of the tagless shirt and give them one.

When it comes to grammar and tags, I really like *question tags*. A question tag is a question added to the end of a sentence. This could either be to keep the flow of a conversation going, to get someone to agree with us, or to ask a question. Here are some examples:

You don't think I can slam dunk a basketball, do you?

He's trying to bring back the sleeveless turtleneck, isn't he?

Interestingly, if the initial statement is positive, the question tag is negative; conversely, when the initial statement is negative, the question tag is positive.

You never learned the Macarena, did you?

---

2   I'm a dad, so I'm obligated to slip in a dad joke here and there.

You put my stapler in Jell-O again, didn't you?

See how that works? Let me rephrase that: you see how that works, don't you?

If the initial statement uses an auxiliary verb (like do, be, or have) or a modal verb (like could, may, or shall), the question tag uses the same verb. I couldn't win the presidential election next year, could I? He sure does like his long ties, doesn't he?

However, if the initial statement doesn't use an auxiliary or modal verb, simply use the verb *do*. The Colts won the game on a last-second field goal, didn't they? Byron didn't buy another apocalypse shelter, did he?

Question tags are fun, aren't they? This is a bit like when you buy a new car: once you're aware of question tags, you'll notice them everywhere. It's kind of like a shirt with an itchy tag: it's annoying, isn't it?

○ ○ ○ ○ ○

Having a nickname for your group of friends

The Rat Pack. The Brat Pack. Hell's Angels. Charlie's Angels. Hootie and the Blowfish. Not only is it awesome to have a cool group of friends, but it's even cooler to give yourself a collective name. It's a noble notion to have these kinds of squad goals. In fact, your posse should start brainstorming these ideas so you can emblazon them on the back of your matching jackets.

I'd get a motorcycle just for the club jacket. Even though I don't know anything about motorcycles or fixing things, I plan on getting a World War II-era sidecar motorcycle for my mid-life crisis. Since my wife has already told me she'll never ride in it, I guess that means I'll finally get the border collie I've always wanted. I'll get him a pair of riding goggles and a sensible doggie helmet. We'll make a great team.

I love collective nouns. A collective noun is a name for the group of similar things. Well-known examples include a pride of lions, a colony of ants, a herd of cows, and a murder of crows. Some of my favorite, lesser-known collective nouns are a tower of giraffes, a business of ferrets, a coalition of cheetahs, and a prickle of porcupines. I will always be disappointed that a group of squids isn't called a squad.

What is the proper term for a group of people? You could accept a number of collective nouns, depending on context: tribe, nation, family, or crowd. But, when it comes to everyday English, how do we refer to our group of friends?

We call them *guys*.

This term, in vernacular usage, applies to a group of male humans, a group of men and women, or a group made up entirely of women. I like this usage not because it's patriarchal, but for the exact opposite reason: calling a group of females *guys* just means that's their posse. Their tribe. Their people.

I argue that *guys* has come to colloquially mean *close friends*. The term can be applied to both men and women. Its popular usage, at this point, is gender-neutral.

Originally, the term *guy* comes from Guy Fawkes, a seventeenth-century rabble-rouser who was involved in the failed Gunpowder Plot in England, in which a group of guys attempted to blow up the members of both Houses of Parliament, King James I, most of the royal family, and leading officers of state in order to establish a powerful English Catholic regime. I'll spare you the rest of the details and cut to the chase: their plan didn't work. Fawkes got caught.

After Guy Fawkes' notorious legend spread, the term *guys* came to be known as something similar to a *gang* or a group of *rebels*—a couple of guys who were up to no good.[3] As the term progressed, its meaning shifted to something more positive, like *people on your team* or *friends you can count on*.

What do you say to your friends if you're trying to get their attention? I would guess most of you would say, "Hey, guys!"

---

3   These guys often started making trouble in the neighborhood. Just ask Jazzy Jeff.

This is in no way the capital *G* grammar rule for a collective group of humans. It's my takeaway based on listening to how people (men and women alike) actually talk today in America.

All the cool kids are naming their squads these days. Just make sure you can secure all the social media handles so you can collectively break the internet with all the likes you get.

○ ○ ○ ○ ○

Some tips for hiring the right milk butler

I need a milk butler. "Need?" you ask, followed by, "What's a milk butler?" Feel free to replace those question marks with interrobangs if you want. If you don't know what an interrobang is, feel free to skip ahead to page 218.

Every morning I eat cereal, then I drink tea. Both activities require adept milk pouring skills, but different kinds of milks. For the record, I go with skim milk in my cereal and whole milk in my Barry's Irish Breakfast Tea.

Have you ever opened a brand new gallon of milk and thought to yourself, "Now what?" Inevitably, you mis-pour the milk and have a cascade of milk down the side of the milk container, only some of which ends up in your bowl. And, when it comes to tea, a milk-pouring catastrophe is the quickest way to end up with way too much milk in your tea. So—yes—I need a milk butler. I just can't afford one yet.

In the same way that I struggle with pouring milk, many people struggle with knowing the right time to use *that* and *which*. I'm just going to hit you with the punchline on this one: if your sentence doesn't need the clause your word (that or which) is joining, use which. If your sentence does need the clause your word (that or which) is connecting, use that. It's as simple as that.

Now for some examples. Here are two nearly identical sentences:

My milk butler's DeLorean, which is painted space gray, gets up to 88 miles per hour quite quickly.

My milk butler's DeLorean that is painted space gray gets up to 88 miles per hour quite quickly.

This is a tale of two sentences. In the first sentence, I implied that the milk butler (whose name is Percy) only has one DeLorean, and it just happens to be painted space gray. The detail about the paint color isn't necessary, so I chose to use *which*. Removing the phrase "which is painted space gray" doesn't change the meaning of the sentence, but simply adds a nice detail to the already intriguing sentence.

In the second sentence, however, you get the impression that Percy owns multiple DeLoreans. The phrase "that is painted space gray" is an example of a restrictive clause; another part of the sentence (My milk butler's DeLorean), depends on it. If you remove "that is painted space gray," the meaning of the sentence changes completely.

Do I need a milk butler? Probably so, but my finances don't yet allow for it. Until then, I'll just have to make sure I'm using *that* and *which* correctly.

What in the word?

Many and *much* are not interchangeable.
Use *many* when the noun you're referring to is countable
(e.g., lightsabers, collectible figurines).
Use *much* when the noun you're referring to is not
countable or quantifiable (e.g., disappointment, sand, wine).

Throw pillows

Sometimes you can have too many of one thing, like presidential primary candidates, for instance. You can have too many toothpaste options at the grocery store. You can also have too many pillows on your bed. Organization expert Marie Kondo is a household name because of her minimalistic outlook. However, you don't want to get rid of all of your pillows, right? You need at least one.

In our writing, we tend to overuse the word *that*. We sprinkle little *thats* into our writing as if they were throw pillows on our furniture. *That* is a conjunction that connects dependent clauses to independent clauses. We need it if a subordinate clause uses conjunctions such as *after, before, because, while* and *in addition to*. For example:

> He said that because he likes hotel waffles so much, he intended to set the alarm clock on his phone before going to bed.

The AP Stylebook instructs us to use *that* "to introduce a dependent clause if the sentence sounds or looks awkward without it." Here are a few examples:

> I think that I am a robot.

> I find that no one believes my robot claim.

Most of the time, we should also use the word *that* after certain verbs, including *assert, declare, make clear, point out,* and *state*:

> I would like to point out that I haven't mentioned Abraham Lincoln up until this point. Now you're thinking about Abraham Lincoln.

Usually, we can omit *that* when a dependent clause follows a version of the verb *to say*. For example:

> Abraham Lincoln said he looked better without a mustache.

Our inclination is probably to insert *that* after *said*. Also, rewrite a sentence if the word *that* appears back-to-back.

What have we learned so far? We only have a few reasons to omit the word *that*. In fact, the AP advises, "When in doubt, include 'that.' Omission can hurt. Inclusion never does." Does this mean we should use throw pillows with reckless abandon? Maybe, but don't tell Marie Kondo. Or perhaps this is a lesson we can apply more broadly to our lives: omission can hurt; inclusion never does.

What in the word?

"Uptick" is an incremental increase.
"Uptake" is the ability to comprehend something.

Descending from Honeycutt's Peak

I think I peaked around age 25, which was longer ago now than I'd like to admit.

When I was a boy, I peeked at my birthday presents because I couldn't wait until the big day.

Understanding grammar has always piqued my interest.

It's time we discussed *peek, peak* and *pique*, three words that sound alike but have different meanings. That makes them homophones, which are words that sound alike but have different meanings and spellings.

Peek means to look or glance quickly, often when you're not supposed to be doing so.

Our neighbors across the street are remodeling their house right now, so I like to peek in the windows to check on their progress.

If you want to remember how to use *peek* correctly, just imagine the two lowercase e's are eyes peering mischievously.
Peak means to reach (literally or figuratively) the highest point of something. In a literal sense, this could be a mountain.

The explorers reached the peak of Mt. Everest this morning.

In the figurative sense, a *peak* is the highest level someone reaches or achieves.

The movie reached its peak when the supposedly unsinkable luxury ship smashed into the iceberg.

To remember *peak*, picture the *a* in *peak* as a capital *A*, thus giving you a visual reminder of a mountain shape.
Pique means to excite or arouse attention or to irritate. I especially like using *pique* as a synonym for *irritate* because I'm a younger brother; in a way, I was born to pique my older sister. Even though we're adults, I still try my best to pique my sister by sending her birthday cards that either make obnoxious noises, or I fill them with confetti, or both. When pique means to excite someone's attention, it's almost like dangling a proverbial carrot in front of someone to intentionally stir curiosity.

The trailer for the new *Space Wars* movie really piqued my interest.

It's good neither to peak too early nor to peek too early; either scenario leads to certain disappointment. Although, be warned: if you peek at your birthday presents before your actual birthday, you're likely to pique the person who gave you the gift in the first place.

For me, life is all about properly managing expectations. If you expect to get your way all the time, you'll certainly be disappointed. On the other hand, I do think you should hope for the best. Instead of rewarding the outcome (which is often out of your control), you should reward the amount of hustle you put into your effort. Instead of half-assing your way into certain misery and then complaining that the world is out to get you, I suggest whole-assing your life and being content knowing you did everything you could to position yourself for success.

If you act as if you've arrived, then you've already peaked, which will only pique those around you. In that case, your only way forward is downward.

○ ○ ○ ○ ○

Being in a band with a cool name

I wish Rustic Citrus was the name of a band I played in back in college. We would have probably been some kind of folk/funk fusion, with banjo, mandolin, and an entire horn section. I would have played cowbell and sung in the Gregorian chanting sections of select songs. But, alas, I wasn't in a band in college; *rustic* and *citrus* are simply two different anagrams for my first name.

Word nerds like you probably already know this, but an anagram is a word, phrase or name with the letters rearranged to spell something else, like *debit card* and *bad credit*. And anagrams, like my credit, have a long history that deserves an explanation.

Anagrams go all the way back to Ancient Greece, first used by either Pythagoras in the sixth century B.C.E. or by the poet Lycophron in the third century B.C.E. Plato and his followers claimed to use anagrams to unlock hidden, spiritual meaning in words and phrases. But my favorite example of anagram nerdiness in history took place long after the Greeks geeked out on switching letters around.

In the 17th century, King Louis XIII enjoyed anagrams so much that he hired an official Royal Anagrammatist named Thomas Billon to entertain his court with the clever rearranging of their names in amusing or mystical ways. Billon was the combination of a jester and obsessive word scrambler. For the record, if anyone's hiring, that sounds like an awesome job for me.

I have some favorite anagrams. For instance, *stifle* is an anagram of *itself*. In Oklahoma (my home state), two cities on the opposite end of the state, *Altus* and *Tulsa*, are anagrams of each other. The brand name *Spandex* was made by rearranging the letters of *expands*. And, I don't want to play favorites here, but an anagram for *Presbyterians* is best in prayer (and also *Britney Spears*).

The book you're reading was published by The County Publishing. Fun fact: *The County* is an anagram for *Honeycutt*. I pretty much self-published this book through a new publishing company I created so it would look as if I wasn't self-publishing. Is that the same thing as money-laundering? I think I need to call my lawyer.

Finally, *eleven plus two* equals *twelve plus one*. Don't let that blow your mind too much. I am considering the pseudonym Mr. Ray Gugam (an anagram of *Grammar Guy*). Is Curtis Honeycutt *hectic unto yurts*? I'll let you decide.

What in the word?

Ripe is when a fruit is ready to eat.
Rife is when something happens over and over again.

I'd love to be in a real band someday, if for no other reason than to come up with cool potential band names. Because it seems like most of the good band names have been taken already,

I'd have to come up with something original and daring. I think I've got it.

Are you ready? Ladies and gentlemen, give it up for Mondegreen!

After a quick Google search, it appears as though both *Mondegreen* and *The Mondegreens* are already band names. Why are all the good ones already taken?

Because I don't want to get in a legal battle with either band, I'll just tell you about the term *mondegreen* instead. A mondegreen is a term for a misheard music lyric that you sing or hear instead of the correct lyrics. Writer Sylvia Wright coined the term in 1954 in an article for *Harper's Magazine,* in which she recounted a misunderstood song lyric from "The Bonny Earl of Murray." Instead of the actual lyrics "...and layd him on the green," Wright heard "...and Lady Mondegreen." In the same article, she concludes: "The point about what I shall hereafter call mondegreens, since no one else has thought up a word for them, is that they are better than the original."

I love mondegreens. Some notable mondegreens include lyrics from Jimi Hendrix's song, "Purple Haze": "Excuse me while I kiss this guy" instead of "Excuse me while I kiss the sky." Pretty much every line from Elton John's "Tiny Dancer" is easy to mishear. "Hold me close now Tiny Dancer" really does sound like "Folding clothes with Tony Danza." I've also heard people think this line said "Happy birthday, private waxer" and "Hold me close, I'm tired of dancing."

Our brains hear these musical words and interpret them as whatever sounds make the most sense. That's why, when we're listening to a Pat Benatar hit, we're prone to hearing "Hit me with your pet shark" instead of "Hit me with your best shot." I think I like the "pet shark" line better.

I could go on and on with examples of familiar mondegreens, but I want to take a moment to dub the already-knighted Elton John as the King of the Mondegreens. There's something about his lyrical cadence that causes our brains to make bizarre connections. In "Bennie and the Jets," instead of hearing "She's got electric boots, a mohair suit," we think we're hearing "She's got electric boobs, and mohair shoes." In "Candle in the Wind," I used to hear "Goodbye enormous jeans" instead of "Goodbye Norma Jean." In "Rocket Man," I thought the line "Burning out his fuse up here alone" was "Burnin' all the shoes off everyone." It almost makes sense.

If and when I create a band, I'll make sure to channel Elton John to confuse fans as to what I'm singing (of course I'll be the lead singer). So, if you ever hear me going on about some guy named "Monty Green," you may want to look up the lyrics to find out what I'm actually singing. Or maybe "Monty Green" will be my stage name. I'll take a page out of Antoine Roundtree's playbook. Perhaps you know him better as a 1990s rapper named Skee-Lo; if you don't, you need to tune your listening device to his 1995 album, *I Wish*.

Let's go back in time for a minute. It's summer, 1995. Skee-Lo's hip-hop smash single "I Wish" is blaring in my ear from one earbud of a shared Sony Discman sporting fresh batteries. My friend Cody has the other earbud. We're riding in the back seat of Cody's parents' car en route to Sweetwater, Texas, for someone's wedding (maybe his cousin—I can't remember). We were memorizing every word to "I Wish"—at least we thought they were the correct lyrics; now I'm seriously second-guessing my ears.

I was invited along, clinging to the simple hope of splashing around in the hotel pool at Sweetwater's Holiday Inn. When we got there, we immediately found the pool...empty. Our dreams were shattered. Now we found ourselves in the middle of nowhere with a cowboy wedding to attend and a hotel pool sans water. Sweetwater? More like no water.

So we had nothing better to do but to memorize each word to Skee-Lo's Grammy-nominated song about wishing he were a little bit taller as well as wishing he were a baller so that he could date a good-looking girl. The song encapsulated everything Cody and I wished for as middle school boys. Well, all that stuff and water in the hotel pool.

It breaks my heart to look back on this fond memory because

Skee-Lo's grammar was wrong. You see, Skee-Lo was exploring a condition that was contrary to fact; he was pondering a hypothetical situation and expressing a wish. He was using the subjunctive mood. So, instead of singing "I wish I was a little bit taller" he should have sung "I wish I were a little bit taller."

Contrast Skee-Lo with Beyoncé, who nails it when she sings "If I were a boy" in her 2008 ballad of the same name. In both Skee-Lo's wish to be taller and Queen B's hypothetical exploration of being male, the sentences should use *were* because they aren't true. Some telltale signs of when it's time to use the subjunctive verb form include sentences starting with *If* or when you see the verb followed closely by *would* or *could*.

While subjunctive verbs expand far beyond *was/were*, the examples containing *was/were* are my favorite. All I know is that if I were in charge of an East Texas hotel in the summer, I'd make sure the pool had water in it.

What in the word?

/

This is a forward slash, not a backslash.
When saying a website address out loud, don't say "backslash."
Either say *forward slash* or simply say *slash*.

I'm nostalgic for the past. As you can tell, my musical tastes are from at least a decade ago. In fact, I collect vinyl records and listen to them on my vintage turntable. I live in a house that was built in 1890. I write a newspaper column, which is something at this point I'll have to explain to my grandkids from our carbon-negative, kale-based colony on Mars. I'm a thirty-something with the soul of an octogenarian. I have a hard time admitting the past has passed.

The words *past* and *passed* are easier to get mixed up than a set of identical twins on school picture day. Their meanings are related, and we don't want to look dumb by confusing the two. *Past* can be an adjective, noun, adverb, and a preposition. Its meaning almost always refers to something that happened before the present time. For example: In the past, MTV played actual music videos. Over the past 12 months, an entire year has gone by. The time is a quarter past four. These uses of *past* all point to a time that happened prior to the present.

Passed is a verb that is the past participle of the word *pass*. It means to move ahead or proceed. For example:

> In his career, Peyton Manning passed for 539 touchdowns, an NFL record.

> Congress passed no legislation last week.

You get the idea.

Here's where things get confusing. You could correctly write "I somehow passed the elephant without seeing him." You could also correctly write "I somehow walked past the elephant without seeing him." The only difference in these two sentences is the word *walked*. As a rule of thumb, use *past* whenever your sentence already includes an active verb like *walked*.

Sometimes "passed" trips us up when it's not used as an active verb. For instance:

> Time has passed since we last met.

> He passed away.

> The local taco restaurant has finally passed its health inspection.

Passed doesn't always indicate literal movement.

Past almost always deals with time. *Passed* almost always deals with movement. The easiest way to remember this is that *past* is a shorter word than *passed,* and time is a shorter word than movement. I just need to make sure I don't get completely left in the past.

○ ○ ○ ○ ○

Checking in: How's it going so far?

You're reading this book. Let me ask you this: at this point, do you love it, or do you really love it? Are you having a hard time understanding if I actually think good grammar makes your life better? I'll answer your question: yes, I really do.

If you don't think this book is funny or remotely chuckle-worthy, feel free to drop the book off at a little free library or, better yet, give it to your friend who has a good sense of humor (she'll love it!).

If you are poised to leave a one-star Amazon review, keep reading—I saved my best stuff for later in the book.

If you're my mom, thanks for buying a whole case of books. I'll sign them all at no extra charge. I promise to call you back soon.

Can we talk about physical and electronic books (e-books) for a second? I like them both for different reasons.

A few years ago I fell hard into the Pinterest fad of organizing my books by spine color. I have a wall of books spanning both the literary and color spectrums. I love a good physical book. You can get it signed by the author. You can collect first editions. You can take in the musky smell of the paper and hear the swish of the cream-colored pages turning. You can loan a book to a friend, which assumes you're prepared to buy a second copy because that friend will probably misplace it. I love books.

I also like e-books. I especially like e-books when I'm reading a new author to whom I'm not ready to swear a physical book allegiance. I like bringing an e-book reader on vacation or on an airplane. An e-book reader takes up less room than multiple books, which means more room for souvenirs. I love my Kindle because I can hard-press on a word and the definition will pop up. Just last night I tapped on the term *maître d'hôtel* to learn that our modern term *maître d'* comes from this original French phrase which directly translates into English as "master of the house." I can't read that phrase without going into the *Les Misérables* soundtrack.

So, if the question is: do I like physical books or e-books? My answer is: yes! I like them both, and I prefer to own physical copies of my favorite books.

○ ○ ○ ○ ○

Like it (or not)

Contrary to what social media tells us, it's not all about the "likes." That brings up a great grammar question: when should you use *like* and when should you use *such as*?

Here's the rule: *such as* indicates inclusion, while *like* suggests comparison. Take this example:

> Curtis has visited states such as Rhode Island, Idaho, and North Dakota.

The *such as* in this sentence indicates Rhode Island, Idaho, and North Dakota are included in the states Curtis has visited. In case you're wondering, all three states do, in fact, exist.

How about this:

> Curtis enjoys limited-edition treats like the McRib.

The *like* in this sentence suggests there are other, comparable limited edition treats Curtis enjoys in addition to the McRib. Take, for example, the pumpkin spice latte or Reese's peanut butter eggs. Why can't we have these things year-round? Although I realize their scarcity adds to their allure, these items are the closest thing to perfection you can get for under four bucks.

Here's the McRub: not everyone agrees. While I prefer clear-cut answers, I'm not finding many in the nuanced English grammar universe. Some linguists think *such as* sounds too formal to our casual eardrums. In our rapidly devolving spelling and grammar multiverse in which we find ourselves, I tip my cap to those whose prose is elegant and purposeful.

If your intentions are to use grammar to be snooty, then I object (like when Starbucks changes their seasonal menu from pumpkin to peppermint). On the other hand, if you've got it, flaunt it (like if you ingeniously chose to save a pack of Reese's eggs in the vegetable drawer of your refrigerator for six months, you deserve to enjoy them in January).

While this issue seems to involve a minor, hair-splitting distinction, you've got to love good grammar; after all, it's only available for a limited time.

Things People Don't Like

Crazy conspiracy theories

I have a friend who, for purposes of this book, we'll call "Byron." He and I are both intrigued by conspiracy theories. The primary difference between Byron and me in our love for conspiracy theories is that he believes at least a few of them. Not only does he believe Paul McCartney died in a November 1966 car crash, only to be replaced by some bloke called William Campbell; Byron also believes that we faked the moon landing. These theories couldn't be further from the truth.

How do we distinguish between *further* and *farther*? The easiest way to decide which word to use in your specific syntactic situation is this: use *farther* when you're referring to physical distance and *further* when you're describing figurative or metaphorical distance. What's great is that *farther* has the word *far* in it, and you already know that *far* deals with physical distance.[4]

I'll share a hypothetical example: suppose Rick and Gary are flying to the moon in order to prove that we've never been there and that the moon landing was a massive, deep state government coverup. For the record, I do not subscribe to that opinion, but Rick and Gary do. They've built a space vessel, successfully rocketed out of Earth's upper atmosphere, and are now cruising weightlessly toward their lunar destination. Gary, who is chronically impatient, turns to Rick, the pilot of the ship, and asks, "Rick! Are we there yet? How much farther?" Gary is referring to a physical distance, so *farther* is correct.

Later in their journey, Rick and Gary are passing time by discussing various conspiracy theories. As Gary rambles on about how lizard people actually built the pyramids, he remarks, "Rick! Don't you get it? How much further down the rabbit hole can we go?" While on the one hand, you could argue that a rabbit hole is a physical distance, in this instance the rabbit hole Gary refers to is figurative, so *further* is correct.

On the bright side, if it's unclear which word to use because you can't determine if you're referring to physical or figurative distance, most experts agree *further* and *farther* can be used interchangeably. And, when in doubt, as a general rule, use *further* because *farther* is more restrictive.

I wish I didn't have to dedicate so much of this book to debunking conspiracy theories. In a study published in the June 2019 issue of *Applied Cognitive Psychology*, D. Alan Bensley and his co-researchers found that people who believe in conspiracy theories are more susceptible to believing pseudoscience and paranormal phenomena. Byron and I constantly argue over the existence of sentient lifeforms on other planets. As you might assume, he believes in aliens and I don't. While I'm on the subject of conspiracy theories, I'll share another one to illustrate another grammar lesson.

---

4 For the record, *further* has nothing to do with *fur*...as *far* as I know.

Paul McCartney is totally alive

Did you know that "I Am the Walrus" was the B-side to The Beatles' 1967 single "Hello, Goodbye?" Usually, a B-side served as a virtual throwaway for a band—a discarded song that would never get radio airtime. The focus was always intended for the A-side to shine. When I learned this piece of Beatle trivia, I was beside myself. Does anyone besides me feel the same way?

Let's take a look at *beside* and *besides*. The two words are often used interchangeably, even though they have distinct intended usages. Let's start with *beside*, which is almost always used as a preposition that means *next to* or *on the side of.* For example:

> I sat beside my record player while trying to dissect the meaning of Lennon's kooky lyrics.

> When singing harmonies, Paul and George often stood beside each other and sang into the same microphone.

I think you get the idea.

Occasionally *beside* means *in comparison with.* Here's an example:

> As The Beatles' songs gained more popularity, they earned their place in rock and roll history beside greats like Elvis Presley and Chuck Berry.

This usage of *beside* is more figurative, instead of being literally next to Elvis and Chuck Berry.

Besides can be used as either an adverb or a preposition. As an adverb, it means in *addition to, also* or *otherwise.* For example:

> My friend Byron believes Paul McCartney died in a car crash in early 1966; besides, he'll buy into just about any conspiracy theory.

As a preposition, "besides" means "in addition to" or "except." For example:

> "Besides the clues on the cover of *Abbey Road*, there's evidence in countless Beatles lyrics to prove the theory," Byron argued.

How are we supposed to tell the difference? No, I'm not referring to Paul McCartney and his supposed impostor/replacement William Shears Campbell (a.k.a. Billy Shears); I'm referring to *beside* and *besides*. Let's stay on topic, here. The easy way to remember when to use *beside* or *besides* is that *besides* has one additional letter in it, and it also means *in addition to*. Use the longer word when you mean *in addition to*. Just like Paul McCartney (who is 100% alive) doesn't want to be accused of being an imposter, don't let people think you're a grammar wannabe; know the difference between *beside* and *besides*.

○ ○ ○ ○ ○

A diva in the a capella group (every group has one)

What's your position on listening to Christmas music before Thanksgiving? Do you dare deck your halls prior to dressing your turkey? Regardless of what time of year you find yourself reading this, the topic of "when it's okay to listen to Christmas music" poses an existential threat to our modern society and, frankly, I think it's time we put this baby to bed. Let's discuss the appropriate time to Christmas-fy your life as we discuss the proper use of *between* and *among*.

Use *between* when you want to discuss two or more specific, individual things:

> When it comes to December holidays about which I know the least, I have a tricky time choosing between

Boxing Day and Finland's Independence Day.

Although, after looking it up, I learned Finland will be celebrating 100 years since it declared independence from Russian rule.[5] Way to go, Finns.

Use *among* when you want to discuss things that aren't specific or individuals:

> I chose among my collection of obscure Christmas ornaments to find one that made me chortle heartily.

Use *among* when you are discussing a group of people:

> Differing positions on when to begin listening to Mariah Carey's 1994 album *Merry Christmas* caused a major divide among my dance troupe, ultimately leading to its acrimonious disbanding.

Use *among* when you're discussing a person's relationship with a group of people:

> After my amateur dance troupe Twilight Twinkle Toes broke up, I felt like the odd man out living among my former dance pals, who were also my roommates. As it turns out, they just wanted to kick me out of the crew because of my stance on listening to Christmas music exclusively after Thanksgiving. The rest of the group met among themselves and re-formed, calling their new group Bad Blood. I should mention at this point that all our dances were vampire-themed.

Depending on your usage, employing *between* or *among* when referring to location can change the entire meaning of a sentence:

---

5   Source: Google search. Thanks, Dr. Google.

The Woody the Woodpecker balloon in the parade floated *among/between* the marching bands.

Using *among* insinuates Woody's transporters lost control and let go of his strings, while using *between* indicates the parade entries appeared in an orderly fashion. And who appears at the end of the parade? Santa. And, because Santa ends the Macy's Thanksgiving Day Parade, according to logic, it only makes sense to listen to Christmas music after Thanksgiving. I rest my case.

○ ○ ○ ○ ○

Amateur taxidermists

It's time we talked about taxidermy. You've made it this far into a book on grammar usage without any discussion of taxidermy. For that I apologize. I used to date a girl whose dad was an amateur taxidermist. That's God's honest truth. I can sincerely say I was terrified that if I looked at him the wrong way, he'd decorate his den with my corpse. That sounds morbid; but now that I'm a dad of two young kids, I appreciate a parent who can strike fear into his child's significant other. I hesitate to bring up the girl I dated whose parents were both undercover cops. When I showed up for our first date, her mom was routinely cleaning her gun. I was definitely terrified of them both. Fortunately, my wife's dad is merely a county judge who could put me away in the clink indefinitely and no one would ever hear from me again. I guess I'm drawn to people whose parents can make me disappear, so to speak.

Let's talk about a type of word which, in English, only offers three choices. Yes, it's time to learn about articles. And, when I say "articles," I'm not talking about the Greek god of creative painting, Articles (okay, I just made that up). Instead, I'm talking about special kinds of adjectives that are always used with, and give some information about, a noun.

In English, we have three articles: *a, an,* and *the. A* and *an* are considered indefinite articles, which refer to any member of a group. Remember, *a* and *an* = *any.* Use *a* before words that begin with consonants. For example:

> The cat had a fifth leg which dangled freely on the left side of her body.

Use *an* before words that begin with vowels. For example:

> Lance is an amateur taxidermist, specializing in stuffing animals that have extra limbs.

In contrast, English's lone definite article (the) comes before a noun when you're referring to something specific and precise. It makes sense that we have one definite article; it's the only one. For example:

> Have you shaved the dog?

In this instance, you're not referring to just anyone's dog (your neighbor might not be happy if you showed up and shaved his dog); you're referring to *the* dog—probably yours.

When referring to a noncount noun (a noun that usually can't be expressed in a plural form), use *the* or omit the article altogether:

> The juice squirted out my nose when I heard the punch-line (some specific juice, maybe the orange juice you just juiced that morning). To make matters worse, I spilled juice all over the floor (any juice).

When referring to a count noun (a noun that can be expressed in plural form, usually with an *s*), use *a* or *an:*

> I needed a new glass of juice after the earlier incident.

Here, *a* modifies the noun *glass*.

Certain types of nouns do not take an article. These include names of sports (curling, gymnastics, synchronized swimming), names of languages and nationalities (Canadian, Ghanaian, Swedish), and names of academic subjects (history, mathematics, botany).

I could probably devote several more articles to articles. I'm not sure if I even scratched the surface on them. I certainly scratched a surface, but definitely not all of the surfaces. You get what I mean.

○ ○ ○ ○ ○

Picking your friend's nose

> *If anyone corrects your pronunciation of a word in a public place, you have every right to punch him in the nose.*
> —Heywood Broun, journalist

Believe it or not, correcting other people's grammar isn't going to win you any friends. And you might also have trouble keeping the friends you do have if you follow them around with your figurative red pen poised in conversations.

I'll admit, I fell prey to the low-hanging fruit of correcting a friend's grammar the other night. My red ink came out almost as a grammatical reflex. For the record, I was right. Also, for the record, I'm sorry I did it. Unless someone gives you explicit permission to correct their grammar during conversations, just don't do it. You'll look like a jerk. It's almost as bad as picking your friend's nose. You wouldn't do that, would you?

I chose to lay down the grammar hammer over the words *obtain* and *attain*, two word cousins people often get confused. Let's learn about these two words and how to use them correctly. *Attain* is a verb that means to achieve or accomplish reaching a goal. *Obtain* is a verb that means to acquire or get something. Just based on these two definitions, the words seem strikingly similar.

When you consider *attain*, think about achieving or accomplishing something. This is usually something that isn't physical, like enlightenment or wisdom. You can attain a rank in the Army, which isn't necessarily something you can physically hold. When you *obtain* something, it's usually a physical object, like car keys or a pet octopus.

The fine line between attain and obtain is found with things such as degrees and diplomas. You *attain* a degree (something you achieve or accomplish). You *obtain* a diploma (the physical piece of paper). When you *attain* something, it's achieved with a high degree of work and effort. When you *obtain* something, you take ownership of a physical object. In *National Treasure*, Nicolas Cage's character obtains the Declaration of Independence. By doing so, he attains criminal status.

Do you see the difference?

If you choose to correct people's grammar publicly, you risk attaining a reputation for being someone nobody wants to be around. You might even obtain a black eye. So, put the red pens away; people aren't friends with you because they like it when someone points out their grammar discrepancies.

○ ○ ○ ○ ○

Who are you calling an idiom?

Some people take things literally. Kleptomaniacs take things, literally.

Literalists aren't fans of idioms. Idioms are phrases with figurative meanings; they aren't intended to be taken literally. Believe it or not, my friend, Byron, tends to take things literally; so, when I suggest we "paint the town red" on Friday night, he goes to his garage to get his paint rollers.

In fact, poor Byron really has an ax to grind with idioms, although, if I told him that, he'd claim he only had a problem with idioms. Idioms are designed to express a sentiment, feeling, or an idea. If I said, "Don't count your chickens before they hatch," I'm not claiming to be a chicken or egg farmer; instead, I'm suggesting that you shouldn't count on something before it has come into reality. In the same way, when I say, "Curiosity killed the cat," I'm certainly not suggesting that NASA's Mars Rover murdered a cat; I'm suggesting that it's dangerous to be too curious.

An idiom is a type of figurative language. The point of figurative language is to make your speech or writing more compelling or effective. Other types of figurative language include euphemisms, metaphors, similes, hyperbole, personification, and (my favorite) puns. In fact, idioms exist in most languages. This isn't just another tricky English construction that makes our language hard to learn.

One of my favorite idioms is "You can't judge a book by its cover." While I don't agree literally with this statement, its figurative truth holds up to scrutiny. We shouldn't judge people at face value; instead, we should look "under the hood," so to speak, and get to know them better before we draw any conclusions. Feel free to judge my book by its cover; I'm quite happy with the design work by my friend Patrick, an artist who lives in London.

The only literal thing that costs an arm and a leg is going swimming with hungry sharks. As an idiom, however, something that costs "an arm and a leg" is merely incredibly expensive. The same idea goes for "robbing the cradle." You're not stealing a baby, but instead, when someone says this she means that you are marrying someone significantly younger than you.

Idioms are a dime a dozen, so forgive me if I rubbed you the wrong way; please don't get bent out of shape. Sometimes it's hard to wrap your head around figurative language.

> ## What in the word?
>
> *Exacerbate* is to make a bad situation worse.
> *Exasperate* is to irritate to the point of anger.

Trying too hard

People can sniff out a poser from a mile away. When you try to be cool, you've got to be careful. If the latest fashion craze involves sleeveless turtleneck rompers, you've got to ask yourself: Do I look good in sleeveless turtleneck rompers? If you decide to adorn yourself with a sleeveless turtleneck romper just to look cool but the garment does no favors for your form, it will show. After all, rompers don't lie. If you're trying too hard, your ploy is likely to backfire.

Should you say *try and* or *try to* look cool? That's another topic of discussion altogether.

Of course, they were gonna try and kill me. Do not try and bend the spoon. Thor, you gotta try and bottleneck that portal. I just quoted the movies *Riddick*, *The Matrix*, and *The Avengers*, respectively. I could have used more than a thousand other movie quotes to illustrate the fact that the phrase *try and* is a fixture of popular culture and usage.

This question begs to be answered: just because it's popular, is the *try and* trend okay? We certainly live in a post- "proper" society. No longer do we dine in the parlor or take tea on a doily on a regular basis. Does that mean rules don't apply anymore? Does that mean grammar relativism is a slippery slope to the land of doofus textspeak chaos? Let's pump the brakes for a second and examine *try and* and *try to*.

Usually, people say *try and* when they should technically say *try to*:

I'm going to try to fix my turntable.

I'm going to try and fix my turntable.

In these two examples, *try to* is considered standard usage, while *try and* is informal or idiomatic usage that means *try to*. However, upon further examination, *try and* may communicate something different. If I *try and* fix my turntable (which is broken, by the way...I'm devastated), it implies that I will be successful in fixing it.

I will try and pass my test.

I will try and reboot the server.

In other contexts, *try and* implies irony and suggests certain failure:

"I'd like to see you try and stop me, Batman!"

I'll go ahead and insert my caveat refrain: it's best to avoid using *try and* in a formal context, unless you intend to use it in a literal sense. While filling out the form to nominate my writing on grammar usage for the Pulitzer Prize (thank you, by the way), opt for *try to*, as in:

Honeycutt will try to make grammar palatable through his use of attempted humor; whether he succeeds or not is up to what each reader finds chuckle-worthy.

If you understand *try and* as an idiom (which is a type of figurative language), then go ahead and use it. After all, idioms aren't meant to be taken literally. Technically, *try and* is not standard usage, but I can't try and make you stop using it; in the same way, I can't try and stop you from wearing a sleeveless turtleneck romper. At the end of the day, you're in charge of making your own questionable life decisions. Just do us all a favor and don't show up in one of those "Florida Man" headlines. Don't get the alligators drunk, for God's sake!

○ ○ ○ ○ ○

Comparing yourself to God

Speaking of God, John Lennon famously got in trouble in August 1966 when an interview from March of the same year dug up a single quote where he stated that The Beatles were (at the time) "more popular than Jesus." Although this quote from a March interview was out of context, it led to many former fans burning Beatles records in big, radio station-backed bonfires. This Beatles backlash even led to some credible death threats during their 1966 U.S. tour, which was one of the reasons The Beatles stopped touring at the end of that year.

For the record, I'm a huge fan of both Jesus and The Beatles, but that's not what we're talking about today. Now I'd like to discuss what to do with possessive proper names that end with the letter *s*. Not only do we need to know whether or not they need an apostrophe and an *s* after them, but we also need to know how to pronounce them. We can work it out.

Let's think of some proper names that end with *s*: Jesus, Beatles, Kansas, Curtis, and the lesser-known Greek philosopher Apostrophes (the last one is fake, but otherwise that is an excellent list). When we talk about the sandals that belonged to Jesus, how do we write it? Is it *Jesus' sandals* or *Jesus's sandals*? As usual, it depends on whom you ask.

The AP Stylebook (which is the gold standard for newspaper writing) states that an apostrophe on its own is enough, while the Chicago Manual of Style prefers the apostrophe followed by *s*. So, AP would write *Jesus' sandals* while Chicago would write *Jesus's sandals*. Because I usually write for newspapers, I tend to agree with AP style.

How do you pronounce these words? I'm a fan of pronouncing

words like they're written. The Beatles' music inspired the new movie *Yesterday*. When saying this sentence aloud, I would say "Beatles," not "Beatles-ez." Similarly, I prefer "Jesus' sandals certainly logged many miles as he visited several ancient cities." I would pronounce the possessive name "Jesus," not "Jesus-ez." Not everyone will agree with me here, but it's not something over which I'd break fellowship and start a new denomination.[6] If you disagree with my all-or-nothing approach, I encourage you to simply "let it be."

○ ○ ○ ○ ○

Saving seats at the movie theater

Did you know that The Beatles' album *Let It Be* is technically a soundtrack? It accompanies the 1970 documentary of the same title. If the film came back to theaters, I would probably go see it by myself.

You see, I don't attend many movies with groups anymore. Part of that is a life stage issue—most of my friends are married and have small kids. It's hard to justify the added babysitter expense if we want to go out for the evening. Before that, I was always the guy who arrived early. Because of my promptness, I ended up saving seats for the whole group. I'd start declaring my group's territory by draping my jacket over a pair of seats. Then I'd put my popcorn and drink in the cupholders a few seats away.

As the minutes ticked on, I'd have to fend off more people who also wanted *middle middle* of the theater. The anxiety of saving six to eight seats for my friends who were chronically five minutes late ended up being too much for me; I did not like this setup one bit.

That brings me to the crux of some more important grammar guidance: what's the difference between *setup* and *set up*?

---

6 Isn't this who the Essenes were? Bible grammar joke!

Let's start with *setup*. Use *setup* (or *set-up*) as either a noun or an adjective. As a noun, *setup* means the arrangement or organization of something. For example:

> The camera setup was all wrong, so the director kept adjusting the shot.

As an adjective, *setup* often gets used in technology situations:

> Go to the setup screen to change your network settings.

As a verb, use *set up*:

> I set up my friend Byron with his new job answering phones at the conspiracy theory hotline.

> We set up our robot so it would never attack humans.

Think about it this way: the verb version of the word spreads out. It is in motion; it stretches and moves. The noun version (*setup* or *set-up*) is compact. It's a box—a static thing.

Interestingly, you can apply this same model (noun and adjective vs. verbs) to other sets of words. Some include *workout* and *work out*, *makeup* and *make up*, *dropout* and *drop out*, and *checkout* and *check out*. When used as a noun or an adjective, these words are either one word or one word with a hyphen; when used as a verb, these words are two words.

Now that movie theaters have a different setup (with seats you reserve ahead of time), I don't have to be so upset all the time. After all, the most important part of the movie is during the last five minutes, when they set up the perfect conditions for yet another sequel.

○ ○ ○ ○ ○

What in the word?

Premier is something that is the highest in rank.
Premiere is the first showing of a movie or performance.

Bucking fashion trends

Have you ever seen a picture of yourself from an unusual angle? You look at the photo and realize, "Who is that person? Oh... that's me. I do *not* like what I see." You hardly ever see the back of your head and—when you do—you vow to wear hats from that point forward. Or maybe you realize your favorite corduroy jacket is doing you zero favors when it comes to the looks department. In fact, this jacket makes you look like a stupid, corduroy hippopotamus.

Using the wrong word is kind of like that, even when it's the trendy thing to do. Sometimes we unknowingly use a popular buzzword regardless of whether or not we understand its meaning. I'd like to discuss a trend I've noticed when it comes to the use of the word *reticent*. People are starting to use *reticent* when they should be using *reluctant*. Let's get it straight, shall we?

Reluctant is an adjective that means unwilling to act. We get this English word from the Latin *re-* (against) and *luctari* (to struggle or wrestle). So, *reluctant* literally means to struggle or wrestle against something. It has to do with action. Here's an example:

> Because Steve always took good care of his things, he was reluctant to spring for the AppleCare plan on his new iPhone.

Reticent is an adjective that means disinclined to speak.

Breaking it down into the original Latin, we get *re-* (in this case, *re-* means *once more* or *again*) and *tacere* (be silent). Reticent, therefore, means *to be silent again*. We get the word *tacit* from this Latin word. Here's an example:

> Since Sheila's such a humble person, she's reticent to comment on her recent promotion.

Lately, people have begun using *reticent* when they mean to say *reluctant*. For example, I've heard someone say something to the effect of:

> I'm reticent to RSVP for Glen's birthday party this year, especially if he's going to do his idiotic magic act again.

In this case, *reticent* is not the right word to use. Instead, stick with *reluctant*. Also, go to Glen's party; you're one of his only friends. Humor him and clap when he pulls those dinky flowers out of thin air.

Just like wearing a trendy corduroy jacket could actually backfire on your high fashion status, using a trendy word in the wrong way is a bad idea. The next time you're in the dressing room at your local clothier's, don't be reluctant to take a picture of yourself in the mirror from a crazy angle—you don't want to end up on the worst-dressed list in your local gossip magazine.

○ ○ ○ ○ ○

Pleated pants

I'm sure pleats will eventually come back into style. I still remember the pleated khakis I wore to church in the mid-1990s. My Dockers brand double-pleated pants complemented my penny loafers to perfection in order to create that "nice-Baptist-guy-all-the-girls-just-want-to-be-friends-with" look I was going for. When pleats became passé, I traded my Dockers for blue jeans, much to my parents' chagrin.

Right now I don't want to talk about pleats; instead, I'd like to take a look at the words *pleaded* and *pled*. As I write this, you can't turn on the TV without hearing about high profile political court cases. Because of this, I think it's a great time to brush up on the different ways people claim their innocence while under oath.

Back in December 2018, former personal lawyer to President Trump Michael Cohen said, "I take full responsibility for each act that I pled guilty to—the personal ones to me and those involving the president of the United States of America." Yet at the end of January, a New York Times article led with this line: "President Trump's longtime adviser Roger J. Stone Jr. pleaded not guilty on Tuesday..."

Is it possible both usages are correct? If the past tense of *lead* is *led*, and if *bleed* becomes *bled*, shouldn't the past tense of *plead* be *pled*? Not so fast! What about *bleat* and *bleated* or *knead* and *kneaded*? There's no pattern to this word construction, so let's seek an expert opinion. According to both the AP Stylebook and the Chicago Manual of Style, *pleaded* is always the acceptable past tense form of *plead*. They assert that *pled* is considered a colloquialism, which is a really nice way of saying "bless your heart, you don't know any better."

When it comes down to it, *pled* isn't incorrect, but it's certainly losing in the popularity polls. According to Google Books' Ngram Viewer, pled has gained considerable popularity in recent years when it comes to appearances in books, but pleaded still outpaces pled by a steep margin. So, while AP and Chicago Manual of Style would like you to believe that *pled = dead*, people like Michael Cohen use *pled* perhaps more often than we think. And, if the federal investigators keep handing out subpoenas, we'll all be paying attention to how each individual pleads (and also if his/her pants have pleats).

○ ○ ○ ○ ○

Talking politics at a dinner party

Stay in your lane, Grammar Guy. Grammarians shouldn't talk politics.

You've heard about the three conversation topics to avoid in polite company: money, religion and politics. But what about these taboo subjects as they relate to grammar? I hope your grammar is rich, and that when your friends hear your eloquent prose they'll imagine baby angels playing harps because you're so close to God. Politics is another story.

Former Speaker of the U.S. House of Representatives Tip O'Neill famously said, "All politics is local." What I want to know is: is all politics singular or plural?

It depends.

Politics is/are a noun that can either be used with a singular or plural verb. Like a tie-breaking legislative vote, *politics* can go either way. The following rules we discuss for politics can be applied to any of the -ics family of academic words: *mathematics, ethics, optics, economics, physics,* et. al.

Most of the time, politics is used as a singular noun. Here are a few examples: One of my least favorite things to talk about is politics, especially with my family. Talking politics makes Thanksgiving dinner uncomfortable and awkward for most families. Politics is a dirty business.

Politics can, however, be plural when referring to a specific set of beliefs. Here are some examples:

> Uncle Lance's politics are bonkers, especially after he knocks back a few boxes of wine.

> My politics have evolved in a particular direction over the years, but I'll try to keep them to myself.

> Do you believe how mainstream her politics are? She'll never make it through the primaries in this political climate.

Whether politics is singular or plural, conservative or liberal, one thing's for sure: American politics is a tricky subject to navigate these days. If you share your political opinion, you open yourself up to vitriolic anger from whomever espouses the opposite position on that issue. On the other hand, if you stay quiet, you may come across as apathetic.

My solution? Hang out as often as possible with people who don't think, look, dress, or talk as you do. Embrace honest, respectful conversations about your similarities and differences. You're likely to realize you have more in common than you think you do.

○ ○ ○ ○

It's hard to win at life when you're losing

We all prefer to win. Right now I'm teaching my son the valuable lesson about how to be a good loser. As much as I want to let him win every once in a while, I don't go easy on him in any skill-based game. However, when it comes to games that involve no skill whatsoever, he beats me all the time. He kills me at Trouble. He destroys me at Chutes and Ladders. I don't even want to talk about playing Hi Ho Cherry-O. Nobody likes losing, but sometimes we can't control whether we win or lose.

Here's a brief record of things I have lost in the past month: keys, a charging cable for my phone, chapstick, patience, earbuds, wallet, sanity, a travel mug, and roughly three more charging cables. Fortunately, I can find or replace most of these things, although I'm still looking for my sanity. If you have any clues of its whereabouts, let me know.

I've received the following question several times over the past few months: can something *go missing*? This phrase *go missing, gone missing,* or *went missing* has crept into American usage over the past few years. Some editors hate it. So, is it correct?

First of all, it's important to note that *go missing* is a popular British import, just like The Beatles, *Downton Abbey*, Simon Cowell, and constant self-loathing. The Oxford English Dictionary lumps *go missing* into a group of various other *go* phrases and expressions such as *go crazy, go public,* and *go viral.* This construction with the word *go* means something is passing into a certain condition. I knew where my keys were, then something happened, resulting in their being lost. Therefore, my keys went missing.

What's the problem with *go missing?* The AP Stylebook would rather you use the words *vanish* or *disappear.* However, *go missing* indicates that something disappeared intentionally, unintentionally, voluntarily or involuntarily, depending on context. "The dog conveniently went missing right before her appointment at the veterinarian" gives you a clue that the dog intentionally went missing to avoid the horrors of going to the vet.

Go missing is idiomatic, which is a fancy way of saying it's a slang term. This gives another strike against using it in more formal writing. However, slang and idiom are the proving ground for future everyday, accepted lexicon. Without slang, we wouldn't have words like *veggie, dude, gross,* and *cool.* These words graduated from informal slang status into common usage.

Personally, I'm a fan of new words and expressions. It means a language continues to evolve and recreate itself. A language wins when it survives and continues in new and relevant forms. Now if I can only teach my son not to rub it in after he wins at Hi Ho Cherry-O, I'd get a parenting win. I wonder where he learned how to be a sore winner?

○ ○ ○ ○ ○

What in the word?

Apart is when something is separated from something else.
A part is a piece of a larger whole.
Ape art is what you get when chimps monkey around
with paintbrushes.

If you can't make friends, watch *Friends*.

> *Joey: All right, Rach. The big question is, "does he like you?" All right? Because if he doesn't like you, this is all a moo point.*
>
> *Rachel: Huh? A moo point?*
>
> *Joey: Yeah, it's like a cow's opinion. It just doesn't matter. It's moo.*

Many of you remember the *Friends* episode entitled "The One Where Chandler Doesn't Like Dogs," in which Joey Tribiani further confuses an already confusing phrase. Many people get *moot point* confused with *mute point*, but Mr. Tribiani adds another (and a hilarious) phrasal faux pas to the list.

The correct phrase, of course, is *moot point*, which is an inconsequential or irrelevant point. *Mute* here certainly makes sense. I think the idea is if you mute something, you can't hear it anymore. But *moot* came first. So, what exactly is *moot*?

Moot is something that is open for debate. It comes from the Old English word *gemot*, which was any legislative or judicial court where people would meet to discuss a matter. A moot point was something that hadn't yet been decided. It's where we get the word *meet* from.

How did something that meant "up for debate" become

known as something trivial and irrelevant? Welcome to Moot Court.

A moot court is where law students competitively hone their arguing skills. It involves a simulated appellate court case, where students focus on the application of the law to a standard set of evidentiary suppositions, facts, and clarifications to which the competitors are introduced. In other words, moot court is made up. The debates held at moot courts are purely academic. Other than a nerdy way for law students to get better at lawyering, the outcomes and arguments make absolutely no real-world difference. They're moot points.

Moot can, therefore, either mean *debatable* or *irrelevant*. In the U.S., it will almost always mean *irrelevant,* while, in England it's more likely to be used as a synonym for *debatable*.

Here's a way to remember moot vs. mute: Since I have two feet, owning only one boot is pointless. *Boot* rhymes with *moot*. A butte is kind of like a mesa. *Butte* rhymes with *mute*. Buttes don't make any noise. One boot is moot. One butte is mute. Just like Joey in *Friends*, I'll be there for you to settle any word disputes or grammar conundrums. If you need me, I'll be at Central Perk sipping giant lattes with Gunther.

Interlude: North Dakota is real.

Do you know anyone from North Dakota? Neither do I. After all, cattle in North Dakota outnumber people by a ratio of more than two to one.

Do you know anyone who has ever been to North Dakota?

While I am intrigued by conspiracy theories, I don't usually subscribe to them. However, I wasn't sure about North Dakota. Sure, everyone knows about South Dakota; it's got the Badlands, Mount Rushmore and the Sturgis Motorcycle Rally. Quick: what's the capital of South Dakota?

It's Pierre (pronounced *peer*). I learned about this pronunciation from a *Where in the World is Carmen San Diego?* soundtrack cassette by the O.G. a capella group, Rockapella, back in 1992.

Back to North Dakota. Unless you have a specific reason to travel to "The Peace Garden State," you might subconsciously assume that South Dakota simply blends northward into Southern Canada. Is it a real place, or is it a massive cartography conspiracy?[1]

That's why I decided to go to North Dakota.

---

1 If you really want to get into North Dakota conspiracies, Google "The Pyramid of North Dakota." You'll learn about some interesting Cold War-era nuclear missile defense sites, and North Dakota's outsized role in nuclear missile defense. I'm not making this stuff up.

My friend Tyler and I actually traveled to North Dakota to find out if it was real or not. Coincidentally, flights to any airport in North Dakota from Indianapolis were ridiculously expensive. Because we were on a shoestring budget in our quest, we bought tickets to Minneapolis, rented the cheapest jalopy we could find, and drove three-and-a-half hours to the state in which Teddy Roosevelt supposedly spent considerable time as a cattle rancher.

As we drove northwest on I-94 through Minnesota, I watched my phone's GPS closely. I didn't want my blue dot to suddenly disappear once we entered the landlocked Bermuda Triangle known as North Dakota. When we crossed the border into Fargo, North Dakota, Siri confirmed that we were, in fact, in North Dakota.

After I met with the director of tourism for Fargo, Tyler and I attended a peewee hockey tournament, toured a local zoo and made snow angels in a pile of plowed snow in a parking lot. When in Rome, I suppose. In all seriousness, if you are leery or suspicious of something's validity, test it. Pry, dig and investigate until your curious thirst is sufficiently quenched. Because I had my doubts about North Dakota's existence, I decided to go there. I concluded that the state that brought us Lawrence Welk, Wiz Khalifa and Phil Jackson does, in fact, exist.

○ ○ ○ ○ ○

I didn't wear glasses until college, which was before I believed in North Dakota. During a lecture hall class, I found myself squinting to see the chalkboard at a distance. After seeing an optometrist, I realized my vision wasn't that great. As it turns out, I'm near-sighted.

Now I wear glasses all the time, even when viewing things up close. Mostly, it's because I want to appear smart. Here comes the segue!

Do you know another way to look smart? Know the difference between *sight, site* and *cite*! These three homophones trip up people all the time, just like when you walk down a flight of stairs, get to the bottom, then try to walk down one more stair that isn't there. It's an awkward and sometimes painful experience.

Sight can either be a noun or a verb. As a noun, it can take many definitions, most notably the ability to see, something worth seeing, or a device that aids your eye. As a verb, *sight* means to view, glimpse or aim at something.

> Those new glasses really helped my sight.

> You haven't lived until you've seen the sights in North Dakota.

Remember, you need to have light to have sight. Sight is all about seeing something. *Light = sight.*

Site can also be a noun or a verb. It has everything to do with location. Site can mean the physical location or position of a building or city:

> Even though the movie is called "Fargo," the site of most of the filming was in the Minneapolis-St. Paul area.

> The town of Rugby, North Dakota, is the site of the geographical center of North America.

When we're talking about electronic position, site refers to websites. A website is something you go visit on the internet. *Site = location.*

Cite is the odd man out of these three words. Not only does it start with a different letter, but it can only be used as a verb. It means to refer to something, to summon someone to come to court, or to deliver a violation.

> The policeman cited me for driving 95 miles per hour outside Bismarck, North Dakota. I thought speed limits weren't a thing in North Dakota!

Sight, site and *cite* can be quite the tricky trio of linguistic limbo. Just like wearing glasses, you can pass as a genius by knowing the right sight/site/cite. For the record: North Dakota is real, and it's spectacular.

Crush It at Work

How good grammar will get you promoted from intern to CEO in (approximately) two weeks

"It is within everyone's grasp to be a CEO."
—Martha Stewart

A 2013 Grammarly study found that there is a direct correlation between good grammar and career success. The researchers studied LinkedIn profiles of 100 native English-speakers working in the packaged goods industry. What did they find? Employees who had fewer grammar errors in their profiles reached higher positions in their companies. Fewer grammar errors led to more promotions. Employees who had between six and nine promotions made 45% fewer grammar errors in their profiles than employees who had only been promoted one to four times.

While this is certainly a small sample size, all signs point to *better grammar = more promotions.* Do you want to sip scotch in your high-backed leather executive office chair as you look at the big city through a wall of floor-to-ceiling windows? Up your grammar game. Ratchet up your résumé. I could argue that removing grammar mistakes from your résumé or LinkedIn profile is more important than running a lint roller over your suit to get rid of dandruff before you walk in to your interview.

Or does better grammar correlate with even more than that in a potential employee or CEO candidate? The type of person who nails her grammar may have just the right amount of ambition, drive, tenacity, and initiative to disrupt the entire importing/exporting industry. Someone who won't settle for bad grammar also won't settle for anything less than Six Sigma-style excellence in the workplace.

Good grammar leaves a positive, lasting impression in the workplace; bad grammar sends a message that you're sloppy, undisciplined, or—worse—not very smart. No one wants to do business with someone whom he perceives as a nincompoop.

As an employee or leader in your business, you're a brand ambassador. Like it or not, the way you compose yourself and your sentences represents your company. If your emails are laced with misspellings, bad punctuation and the wrong version of your/you're, you run the risk of losing clients. Whether you like it or not, you are a writer.

If you're a job seeker, you represent your own brand. Obviously, you want to put your best foot forward; one of the best ways to do that is by improving your written and oral communication skills.

Do you want to nail your interview? Nail your grammar.

Do you want to crush it at work? Crush your grammar errors into a fine dust underneath your perfectly-shined boss shoes. In the following pages, you'll learn how to become the king or queen of the corner office.

Climbing the corporate ladder

Do you want to work your way from the mailroom to the corner office? I can tell you've got gumption, kid, so leave it to me. I'll give you some swell advice that'll have you drinking gold-leafed martinis quicker than you can say "Scrooge McDuck doing the backstroke in a roomful of golden coins."

First things first: we need to clear up the common confusion between *latter, ladder* and *later.*

A ladder is a thing your leaf butler climbs to clean out your gutters. It's a tool with a series of horizontal bars called *rungs* that extend upward on affixed, parallel, vertical poles. I assume you understand this, so it's time to move on.

Latter and *later* are a bit more confusing. Not only are the two words one *t* apart in spelling, but their meanings are similar enough to make this pair bewildering to many. *Later* is an adverb that means "after, or subsequent to, the present time." For example:

> I planted some marigold seeds in my window planter box. A few weeks later, I had bright orange flowers blooming.

Latter is an adjective that means "happening at or toward the end of an activity." It also indicates the second of two things or people that were previously mentioned. Thomas Jefferson once wrote, "Were it left to me to decide whether we should have a government without newspapers, or newspapers without a government, I should not hesitate a moment to prefer the latter." Here T.J. uses "latter" to refer to his preference for the second option—newspapers without a government.

Given the option between a Nickelback CD or a Labradoodle puppy, all of your coworkers would prefer the latter as a birthday present. Don't be the lady who gives Nickelback CDs to people for their birthdays; instead, be the puppy-giving coworker.

Furthermore, don't show up to a meeting later than the posted time. Instead, get there five minutes early. Bosses appreciate promptness, which is a sign of respect for their time. Also, if you offer your boss an unopened pack of Skittles, he'll likely love you forever and promote you sooner than later.

When it comes to climbing the corporate ladder, these tips can get you far toward your goal. In addition, using good grammar will make you more popular than the lady who gives out hypoallergenic birthday puppies.

○ ○ ○ ○ ○

How to show them you mean business

You've gone over your expertly-tailored business suit with your lithium battery-powered lint roller in the executive bathroom. You've humbly positioned your luxury watch so it peeks just so outside your shirt cuffs (which are crisp and precisely the right length). Now you're assuming your power stance at the front of the conference room, getting ready to share your big Powerpoint presentation (or—as it's known in startup circles—your "slide deck").

You're about to deliver a crushing dose of Six Sigma business power to the other suits sitting around the conference table who flew in for this meeting in their corporate jets. But, to get the seven-figure multinational merger deal done, you're going to need one more key ingredient: power verbs.

That's right—power verbs. We all know that verbs are action words, but some of them are puny, anemic and overused. If you use weak verbs in your presentation, the overseas investors are going to start yawning and looking at their own (probably Swiss) luxury watches, wondering at which Michelin-star restaurant they should dine later tonight.

Let's take the word *said* as an example. It's boring, yet we drop it in by default into our everyday communication. Instead, consider more powerful verbs like *yelled, demanded, explained* or *insisted*.

Walk is another verb that screams "weak sauce." No one just *walks* anymore, unless you want to walk straight to the unemployment office. Instead, consider using *strut, dart, march, mosey* or *meander*. See what I mean? Talk about *walking* like a boss, and you'll soon be the boss. You can almost smell the rich mahogany of your boss desk, can't you?

Now let's take a look at *look*. No one even gives it a second glance. Instead of *look*, use a more creative, evocative word like *gape, examine, notice, glare* or *stare*.

Finally, let's talk about *talk*. *Talking* is for career mid-level managers (at best). Instead, use a stronger verb like *spout, reveal, divulge, gab* or *mumble*. Power verbs will win you friends and influence people, especially executive corporate vice presidents of overseas fiduciary acquisitions.

Using power verbs will knock the designer socks off your potential investors. Replacing boring, bland verbs with power verbs will give you an instant air of confidence and success. This tactic will win you fans everywhere from the boardroom to the bedroom.

What in the word?

A *phase* is a stage or time period, like the phases (not faces) of the moon.
Faze is when you are disturbed by something.

Invent your own jargon; get promoted.

Verbing weirds language.
—*Bill Watterson, Calvin and Hobbes*

Nod in meetings. Walk around with a clipboard in your hand and a pencil behind your ear. Do the crossword in pen. Wear a leather bomber jacket. These things will make everyone in the office think you've got that sweet C-suite potential. You want to know something else that will turn you into an overnight corporate success? Make up words. Or—better yet—take an existing word and turn it into a verb.

I call this the *verbification* of nouns, which bothers many people (especially the word *impact*). Nouns like *impact, access, text, Google* and *task* have transitioned their parts of speech from nouns into verbs in our recent usage. Is this necessary?

The short answer is no. It seems that the verbification of nouns follows a trend in English usage that can either be viewed as a desire to be more efficient or as simple laziness. On one hand, it's unnecessary to verbify nouns:

The grammar book had a significant impact on me.

In this case, *impact* is a noun, just like the good Lord of the English language intended. In a world where *impact* is a verb, you'd say:

The grammar book impacted me significantly.

While I think I agree that I don't like when nouns become verbified, I think it's just a matter of personal preference. For instance, I'm not a fan of the word *process* as a verb. When someone says something like "I'm really processing a lot of emotions right now," I feel that, while not wrong per se, this makes humans sound like robots.

Originally, *process* was a noun. Then we created room-sized computers which computed the processes we in-putted into them. Soon, in an effort to mince words, we said the computers were processing our punch cards to find funny cat videos on the internet (forgive me if my history is approximate here; I was born in the Orwellian year of 1984).

Now computer processors are powerful enough to provide robot vacuums with artificial intelligence. Am I suggesting the verbification of nouns will ultimately (albeit indirectly) lead to the robot apocalypse? I'm not sure; I think I need to process it some more.

○ ○ ○ ○ ○

Shakespeare's made-up words

I'll be the first to admit I didn't understand or enjoy much of the Shakespeare assigned to me in high school. I hope that doesn't ruin my reputation with my fellow word nerds. On the other hand, I love how Shakespeare invented words that are still common in our modern lexicon, including wormhole, swagger and skim milk. While word scholars now debate how many words he actually came up with, Shakespeare certainly knew a lot of words.

That reminds me of a word duo that often gets mis-matched and misused: *a lot* and *allot*. First, I want to get something out of the way and settled so we can get on with our lives: *alot* is not a word (unless you capitalize it and are referring to the town in India named Alot). The non-word *alot* often gets used instead of *a lot*, which means a large amount or large number. People mistakenly write things like "I know alot about robot movies." In this sentence, the person should have written *a lot*.

Allot is a verb that means to give out, distribute or divide.

It doesn't get used as much as its word cousin *a lot,* but it has its merits.

> Make sure to allot the same amount of Skittles to each child unless you want a riot on your hands.

In this case, an even allotment can save you from a disastrous toddler turf war.

I will say, we use the phrase *a lot* far too often. It's vague and doesn't add much pizzazz to your writing or speaking. Instead, consider words and phrases like *a plenitude, several, heaps, an abundance,* and *scads.* As an adjective, *a lot* is a bland nothingburger (check your dictionary). The more inspiring words are like the little-used exotic spices in your spice rack that add variety and interest to your bowl of alphabet soup. By expanding your vocabulary, you make Shakespeare's ghost proud.

In conclusion: *alot* isn't a word. *Allot* means "to give out." *A lot* means "a large amount," and it's kind of boring. I challenge you to use something more interesting instead; you have a myriad of options.

○ ○ ○ ○ ○

Avoid corporate buzzwords

> *Use the right word, not its second cousin.*
> —Mark Twain, *Fenimore Cooper's Literary Offenses*

Contrary to what *Inc.* and *Forbes* magazines tell you, it's probably time to pump the brakes on corporate buzzwords. Since the dawn of *synergy,* the movers and shakers in the world of business have been coining and cloning their own terms for things. While I appreciate inventing language and playing with words, sometimes stringing together a bunch of overused buzzwords leaves people scratching their heads wondering what you actually meant to say.

I'm a proponent for, as John Mayer sings, "say what you mean to say." Because the term *cutting edge* got tired, people started wanting to be on the *bleeding edge*. That's a little gross, if you ask me. Just say you want to be on top of or ahead of current trends and technologies.

In my brief stint as a marketing director for a software startup, people used the term *slide deck* ad nauseam; sometimes they'd just say *deck*. This is a blatant attempt at making a PowerPoint presentation sound sexy. I recognize that Keynote is a thing, and that Keynote presentations can actually be pretty cool. Keynote presentations are to PowerPoint presentations as the Ken Burns effect is to documentaries. Instead of *slide deck* or *deck*, just say *presentation*. People know what you mean.

I'll lump the next terms into the same category. If I had a dollar for every time I've heard a tech company claim to disrupt the system, rock the boat, or be a change agent for its specific industry, I'd be able to buy my own solar-powered megayacht. Everyone wants to be different, just like everyone else. We all want to *move the needle*. Put your needles away and do your work. As much as we'd all like to make a big splash, companies like Microsoft and Apple weren't built overnight. In fact, I challenge you to look at businesses dubbed *overnight successes*. Most of the time you'll find companies who have built their products and services after a series of failures and years of scraping by. Disruption often takes time.

Allow me to unpack the term *unpack* for a minute. Unpack (and its second cousin, *drill down*) means to analyze, inspect, study, or dissect. Forgive me for *pushing back* against the status quo on this one. *Push back* is merely a nice way of saying *I disagree with you*. We're all grownups, right? I think we can disagree with coworkers in a healthy way; we don't need to dress it up in a buzzword. Not everything has to be buzzworthy or go viral to be a success.

In case you can't tell, I'm not a fan of buzzwords. I think they're weak and oftentimes empty phrases that take away from the message you're trying to communicate. If you're confident in your product or company, you don't need the smoke and mirrors of corporate buzzwords.

What in the word?

Eminent means prominent or famous.
Imminent means something that is certainly going to happen.

Use these verbs to amp up your résumé

Your résumé can be like a key that unlocks the door to an interview for your dream job. Alternately, it can be the thing that prevents you from even getting a phone call. You don't have to have a funky design, neither do you need to attach a pair of Hamiltons to your résumé with a paperclip. Instead, drop in some well-placed success verbs and you'll be on your way.

According to corporate success guru Marc Cenedella, action words aren't enough. Instead, he suggests, you use what he calls "success verbs" to strengthen your résumé. When listing your work history accomplishments, use bullet points. Follow each bullet point with an energetic verb that packs a powerful punch. After each "success" verb, add a specific numerical value for your career accomplishment. That's the basic formula: bullet point, success verb, numerical data.

First, let's focus on some tired, weak verbs that most of us have on our résumés. Words such as *managed, led, established* and *performed* are boring and overused. Just because you did these things doesn't mean you were any good at them. When you do this, you're basically just listing your job description, not your job accomplishments. You need to show that you have excelled in your field; using these verbs does you no favors and does not help you stand out among a crowded field of candidates.

Let's shift our focus to the magical words that can help get you hired. Cenedella lists 25 specific, compelling verbs: accelerated, achieved, added, awarded, changed, contributed, decreased, delivered, eliminated, exceeded, expanded, gained, generated, grew, improved, increased, introduced, maximized, minimized, optimized, produced, reduced, saved, sold and streamlined. These verbs express vigor and translate to bottom-line organizational impact.

Now all you have to do is follow these verbs with a measurable statistic that will impress the socks off your potential employer; easier said than done. While you certainly don't want to suggest anything untrue in your résumé, you should be creative and think of all the ways you had a positive impact on each organization for which you worked. You can write an effective energetic résumé; just ditch that thesaurus and use this list of success verbs instead. It's time to make it happen.

○ ○ ○ ○ ○

Showing up on time for the interview

If having kids has taught me anything, it's that I'm never going to be on time for anything again in my life. At best, I'll be ten minutes late to my destination with at least one person crying and at least one person sporting a fresh, unidentified stain. Sometimes all of those people are me. But if time is all relative, does it really matter? Unfortunately, yes. In our culture of scheduled meetings, being time savvy is important.

I often hear people wondering about *next Thursday*. When a corporate headhunter suggests you have an interview lunch at the steakhouse next Thursday, does she mean *Thursday a few days from now* or *Thursday next week*? Is there a correct way to refer to this? Obviously, if she would have said *this Thursday*, she would mean *Thursday a few days from now*. But *next* is a relative term; there's no general agreement on *next Thursday*. When in doubt, be as specific as possible and try to avoid confusion.

What about a.m. and p.m.? Great question. Some would suggest a.m. stands for *after midnight* and p.m. stands for *post midday*, but that isn't true. These abbreviations are Latin: a.m. is short for *ante meridiem* (before noon) and p.m. is short for *post meridiem* (after noon). A.P. style suggests writing these abbreviations with lowercase letters and periods after each letter (e.g., 8:00 a.m.).

While we still have some time, let's discuss noon and midnight. To avoid redundancy, don't say *12:00 noon* or *12:00 midnight*. You can say, "I left the bar around midnight," but it would be redundant to say, "I left the bar around 12:00 midnight."

Finally, we have to talk about time zones (because you'll inevitably find yourself in one before too long). Most of Arizona doesn't even observe Daylight Saving Time, so why do we need to bother with abbreviations like EDT and EST? EDT stands for Eastern Daylight Time, (roughly spring and summer), and EST stands for Eastern Standard Time, which is approximately autumn and winter. Do we need to specify? Probably not, because it's just confusing. Instead, I suggest using *ET* for Eastern Time, *CT* for Central Time, and so on.

○ ○ ○ ○ ○

Master the laser pointer

Cut out all these exclamation points. An exclamation point is like laughing at your own joke.
—*F. Scott Fitzgerald*

Ancient Romans used all capital letters, no spaces and no punctuation. Can you imagine that? For a civilization that gave us concrete, the book, and the calendar system we still use today, you'd think they would have thrown in a period at the end of a sentence every once in a while.

Legend has it that the exclamation point has its origins in the Middle Ages. At the end of a sentence in which a medieval copyist wanted to indicate or emphasize joy, he would write the Latin word *io*, which means *joy*. Over time, the *i* moved above the *o* and the *o* shrunk small enough to become a point, morphing into the exclamation point we know and love today.

There's an episode of *Seinfeld* where Elaine breaks up with her boyfriend after he doesn't use an exclamation point when writing down a phone message for her. A Plenty of Fish Conversation Nation 2018 survey found that "58 percent of singles say bad grammar is a bigger turn off than bad sex." Especially in an age where texting and messaging account for much of the communication between potential love matches, grammar and punctuation play a significant role in your love life.

So, what's my point, already? Should we use exclamation points or should we practice total exclamatory abstinence, as F. Scott Fitzgerald suggested? According to the AP Stylebook, we should "avoid overuse of exclamation points. Use to express a high degree of surprise, incredulity or other strong emotion."

Here's my point on exclamation points: don't go crazy with them. In the same way that bolding an entire section of text, therefore, makes nothing important, dropping in exclamation points all willy-nilly makes you look like a person who has had a few too many espressos. Never use more than one exclamation point at the end of a sentence; it's just unnecessary. Doing so takes your rhetoric up to Defcon 1 and makes the reader think there's a giant asteroid hurtling toward Earth.

I suggest discussing exclamation point usage early on in a relationship so that you can weed out someone whose punctuation habits are incompatible with yours.

○ ○ ○ ○ ○

How to win the watercooler (or Keurig) chat

Is there a way to win or lose at taking breaks at work? Absolutely, there is. I find it helpful to have a baseline knowledge about most things—from sports to pop culture to politics. If you can toss in an intelligent retort about the Titans' new back-up punter, you will score a proverbial work touchdown and you'll be showered with free lunch offers. You can certainly lose the watercooler chat, because work is a fierce competition (and only shooting stars break the mold).

When it comes to sports teams whose names don't end in the letter *s*, are they considered singular or plural? Would you say "The Jazz is winning the game" or "The Jazz are winning the game?"

This is a tricky one. When it comes to the Indiana Pacers, you would always say, "The Pacers are winning the game" because "Pacers" is obviously plural, therefore the noun takes the plural verb *are*. The same goes for the Panthers, Packers, Pirates and Patriots. You would never say "The Panthers is looking sluggish out there."

When it comes to the official rules of grammar, allow me to punt to the AP Stylebook and the Chicago Manual of Style. Both guides suggest you treat all team names as plural, whether or not the team name ends in *s*. So, this means you should (according to the rules) say "The Heat are winning the game."

But what about soccer? And what about England?

Many soccer clubs go by their city or club name. So you have teams being referred to as merely Liverpool or Watford (for city names), or Arsenal or Crystal Palace (for clubs who were originally named for the sports complex where they began). By the same rule, you hear soccer (or football) announcers say things like "Arsenal are really having a tough go of it today."

So, my big question is: does the same rule apply to your team when you're referring to its location?

When referring to teams, locations, and schools, use singular pronouns and verbs:

> Harvard is bad at football.

Team names always take plural verbs:

> The Crimson are good at math, but lousy at scoring touchdowns.

However, British English sees things differently. The official British rules state a team is always plural, whether you're referring to the team name or the city name. That's why you hear British announcers say, "France are the World Cup champions." This sounds strange to our American English ears because our rules are different.

So, if the American rule makes you develop a nervous tic, simply refer to teams by their city or state:

> New England is in the Super Bowl...again.

Now go out there and win your work break. Show them who's going to be their next boss.

How to decipher a meeting request

You snagged that great job at the hot new tech startup where they play ping pong on electric scooters. Congratulations! Your title is probably something like *Chief Dreamer, Director of Awesome,* or something else vague and millennial-friendly. Now you get an email from the HR director (whose business card reads *VP of Hugs*) which states your paycheck will come biweekly.

Does that mean you'll get paid twice a week or every other week? With the big stack of cash your CEO just raised, they could probably afford to pay you twice a week, but it's more likely biweekly here means you'll get paid twice a month.

Couldn't your company's VP of Hugs have also said you'll get paid *semiweekly*? I've always been confused about the meaning and usage of *bi-* and *semi-*. In general, the prefix *bi-* means two or twice. Think about a bicycle with its two wheels or the bicentennial, which happened in 1976 to celebrate the United States' 200th birthday. *Semi-* means half. A semiprofessional basketball player is somewhere halfway between an amateur and a pro. A store's semiannual sale happens twice per year, or every half a year.

So why all the confusion? Both a *biannual* meeting and a *semiannual* meeting occur twice a year, based on how they're commonly used. I've worked for employers who pay bimonthly (twice a month) and others who pay biweekly (every other week). That's inconsistent, or ambiguous at best.

While vague job titles are all the rage right now, vague meanings for words that describe how often things reoccur are just confusing. This ambiguity isn't new, unlike the weird startup company titles. I recommend getting a job description in writing that spells out what exactly your new company's expectations of you are and specify you want to get paid in U.S. dollars instead of an obscure cryptocurrency your founder invented.

When it comes to how often a meeting happens, try to avoid confusion by saying *twice a week, every other week,* or *twice a month.* Even though you sound like an Ivy League summa cum laude when you throw around words like *semimonthly* or *biannually,* you can quickly confuse people, causing them to take extra trips to the VP of Hugs' office (which doubles as a yoga studio semidaily).

○ ○ ○ ○ ○

Winners write in all caps on the whiteboard

You're a winner. I get it. You eat Wheaties for breakfast with a side of victory bacon dipped in awesome sauce. Although you put your pants on one leg at a time, you close record-breaking transcontinental business deals while you're doing it. Your stock portfolio makes the wolves on Wall Street drool with envy.

Are you not quite to this point yet? Or have you already achieved this high ranking, but you'd like to maintain "top wolf" status in your office? Here's a shortcut to the corporate prestige you seek: write in all caps on the whiteboard.

First of all, you have to make sure there's a whiteboard in every possible meeting space, including the bathroom. Have your assistant or intern bring a portable whiteboard with him everywhere he goes just in case you find yourself in an impromptu stand-up meeting situation. Also, bring your own dry erase markers; there's nothing worse than a weak marker that barely shows up on the board. In any meeting, volunteer to write at the whiteboard as soon as you can. Standing up while others sit automatically gives you a position of power and dominance over your competition. Next, master the art of the all-caps handwriting.

If your handwriting doesn't look like an architect's, then you need to (literally) go back to the drawing board. Practice with your backup whiteboard until you get the stems and ligatures just right. Bold, confident whiteboard handwriting shows everyone else that you're a strong, capable leader. Before you know it, you'll be signing everyone else's reimbursement checks with your distinctive bold strokes.

In emails, however, please avoid writing in all capital letters. WHEN YOU WRITE IN ALL CAPS PEOPLE ASSUME YOU'RE YELLING AT THEM. RECEIVING AN EMAIL COMPOSED ENTIRELY OF CAPITAL LETTERS IS KIND OF LIKE GETTING A RANSOM NOTE SLIPPED UNDER YOUR DOOR THROUGH A BLARING MEGAPHONE (I KNOW THAT'S A MIXED METAPHOR); IT'S CREEPY AND OFF-PUTTING. IT MAKES YOU SOUND LIKE A PUNDIT ON A CABLE NEWS SHOW, SCREAMING YOUR TALKING POINTS OVER YOUR DIAMETRICALLY OPPOSED POLITICAL OPPONENT. IT'S CHAOTIC AND UNNERVING.

The same principle applies to bold letters. Bold letters signify importance. They are designed to stand out against a field of normally-weighted text. If everything is important, then nothing is important. Everything has the same emphasis. You could make a great point, but it's lost on your reader because nothing stands out.

It's okay to be bold, but your electronic conversations don't have to suffer by getting the all-bold treatment. Have strong ideas. Lead with vigor. Be a dynamic, visionary, career-focused honey badger. Just take it easy on the caps and the bolding.

The definition of the word *dynamic* means that the rhythms and cadences ebb and flow. Sure, there's a time and place for making big points. Teddy Roosevelt famously said, "Speak softly and carry a big stick; you will go far." The big stick is used as a last resort. Being an even-keeled leader suggests you operate from a default position of peace; you only have to threaten the "big stick" (a.k.a. using all caps or bolded letters) as your final bargaining chip. Don't play your trump card first.

Writing in all caps on the whiteboard will garner instant regard for your personal brand. Your stock will rise faster than a tech stock on its IPO day. However, if you overdo it in your emails, people will rightfully assume you're a psycho. If you find yourself in a pattern of erratic email behavior, maybe you should consider switching to decaf after your first two pots of coffee.

What in the word?

Former refers to the first item in a list of two things.
Latter refers to the second item in a list of two things.
Remember: *former = first*
latter = last

Don't argue with people on the internet on company time (or ever)

Doesn't it feel good to do battle with someone with whom you don't agree behind the safety of a screen? We jump on Twitter on our smartphones to call someone a loser in all caps. We hide inside our anonymous online identities, rapidly re-sharing the outrage *du jour*. Our TV pundits aren't even in the same room; they lob talking points like hand grenades at each other via satellite.

When is the last time someone changed her mind as a result of this kind of argument? In my opinion, this way of waging war is pointless; you and your echo chamber only feel angrier and more self-righteous as a result. Verbal combat over social media and cable news is pointless. Nobody wins.

Now I want to tackle the dummy subject (also referred

to as an artificial or empty subject), which is a verbal construction that weakens your writing, making it seem vague and nebulous. You find yourself using a dummy subject whenever you use *it* or *there* to start a sentence without referring to the noun *it* or *there* represents. Let me use some examples:

> **Weak:** It seems like everyone's just yelling past each other.

> **Better:** After I watch shows on MSNBC, Fox News, and CNN for an hour, my brain hurts. It seems like everyone's just yelling past each other.

In the second example, *it* refers to *shows* from the first sentence.

There also gets used as a dummy subject:

> **Weak:** There are 37 varieties of pineapples in the world.

> **Better:** The World Fruit Council has identified 37 varieties of pineapples in the world.

The second example is stronger because it provides a source for the fact about pineapples. Without the authority of someone like the "World Fruit Council" (which I just made up), the sentence feels indefinite.

In the same way that arguing from behind the shield of a screen makes our arguments go nowhere, using dummy subjects makes your writing sound uncertain and wobbly.

I don't think we would die if we engaged in disagreements with people face-to-face. In fact, I think a healthy level of conflict sharpens us—as long as we don't resort to calling each other "dummies."

What's the right amount of leaning in?

The phrase *lean in* may be a corporate buzzword, but it's worth discussing. Facebook COO Sheryl Sandberg immortalized the phrase when she wrote a best-selling book entitled *Lean In: Women, Work, and the Will to Lead.* What does *lean in* actually mean?

It's all about posture. If you're slumped down in your chair at work, whiling away the hours until the five o'clock whistle blows, you're not leaning in. Not only are you physically disengaged, but your attitude also suggests that you don't care. However, when you lean forward in your chair, you're more alert and likely to be listening with rapt attention and prepared to insert your own great ideas. That's what leaning in is all about: you're ready to interject your awesomeness into your organization.

Italicized words are the *leaning in* of language. When it comes to fonts (or typefaces, if we're being fancy), *Roman* letters refer to the default, upright letters we type into our emails and word processing software, while *Italic* letters are slanted to the right. When you put certain phrases in italics, it draws attention to them as key words you want to set apart for emphasis. These words are literally *leaning in.*

What happens when you lean in too much? You fall on your pants pockets (which is a diplomatic way of saying you bruise your *derrière*—pardon my French). I'm suggesting that if you constantly give 110%, you'll likely experience burnout. In the same way, if you put your entire email in italics, your reader will have trouble discerning what's important from what's ordinary. I highly recommend healthy margins—on paper and in your work/life balance.

Aside from emphasis, when should you use italics in your writing? Surprisingly, AP style suggests that you don't use italics in titles of magazines or newspapers; instead, simply capitalize them (e.g., Sports Illustrated). The AP dictates that books, films, TV shows, songs, albums, speeches, works of art, etc. don't get italicized, either; instead, surround them with a warm pair of quotation mark hugs (e.g., "To Kill a Mockingbird"). Sacred books, including the Bible or the Koran, do not get italics or quotation marks. So, what gets italicized in AP style? Nothing. Just the facts, ma'am. Chicago Manual of Style and the MLA Handbook suggest that you italicize major works instead of using quotation marks.

I have a hard time with the AP's italics rules. Because my column appears in newspapers, I abide by the quotations-around-titles rule when I send columns to editors—but I don't have to like it. I prefer to italicize major works, as well as words for emphasis, non-English words (such as *derrière*), words reproduced as sounds (e.g., Bees go *bzzzzz*.), and words as words (e.g., I challenge you to use the word *indefatigable* in a sentence.). AP style dictates that we should put quotations around words as words, but I prefer to put them in italics.

If you want to make a big splash at your company, lean in at the right time in the right project. If you want to emphasize certain words in your writing, lean in by italicizing key phrases. Just don't lean in too much or you'll fall on your face.

What in the word?

Four is the only number in English, that, when spelled out, has the same number of letters in the number as its numerical value. In Spanish, the only number that shares the same number of letters as its numerical value is *cinco*.

Power posturing for ladder-climbing bosses

Do you want to hit the fast-forward button on your career? Do you want to collect underlings like baseball cards? If so, I suggest adopting a few fundamental power postures. This is all about making yourself look as big as possible. Wear as many jackets as possible; you'll be sweaty, but your co-workers will fear you. Also, stand like you're trying to scare away a bear in the forest.

My favorite power posture takes some work. Before anyone else gets into the office, make everyone else's chair shorter than yours so you'll look like a giant. It may take some MacGyver ingenuity to accomplish this, but you're destined for greatness. Do what it takes to literally rise above everyone else. Before you know it, they'll all be your subordinates.

Just as it's essential to view everyone at work as a subordinate, it's also crucial to recognize a subordinate sentence clause when you see one. A subordinate, or dependent clause, is a clause that can't stand alone as a sentence, but it adds meaning to a sentence's main clause. The main clause, which is independent, can stand on its own. How about some examples?

I am going to work this morning.

This sentence stands on its own; however, that's not all the information or meaning I intend to convey. Allow me to introduce a subordinate clause:

I am going to work this morning if I can find my keys.

In this sentence, "if I can find my keys" not only doesn't stand alone as a sentence, but it adds some important additional information into the sentence. This clause is a subordinate clause.

The word that introduces the subordinate clause itself is called a subordinator, which sounds like some kind of underwater *Terminator* knock-off movie. Common subordinators include *because, since, if, although, while, before, after, unless* and *until*. If your subordinate clause begins your sentence, always add a comma after the clause. Becoming familiar with these subordinators will make it easy for you to recognize subordinate clauses.

If you want that six-figure check, you're going to have to tower over the mere mortal coworkers who either want to be you or date you. Just like subordinate clauses, they can't stand on their own in the proximity of your sheer awesomeness. Before you know it they'll be re-naming all the *Forbes* lists after you.

○ ○ ○ ○ ○

Be brief, then be done.

If you drive an hour from my house, you can get to an Indiana city named Gas City. If you drive into town, you'll reach the City of Gas City City Hall. Did they have to do this to themselves? I like to think that the person who decided on this name did it in an attempt to be saucy. Yet, today you can visit the City of Gas City City Hall. While this is incredibly repetitive, it's not an example of tautology.

Tautology is a form of repetition where the same thing is said twice using different words. In the City of Gas City City Hall, you're saying the same thing three times using the same words. We get the word *tautology* from the Greek noun *tautologos*, meaning "repeating what is said." The Gas City example is an instance of tautophony, which is the repetition of the same sound.

Here's a sarcastic use of tautology by one of my heroes, Mark Twain: "Suppose you were an idiot and suppose you were a member of Congress. But I repeat myself." In an age of limited bandwidth and diminished attention spans, brevity is not only the soul of wit, as Shakespeare wrote in *Hamlet,* but brevity is the soul of effective communication.

Can you repeat that again? That's a prime example of tautology. How about this one: "It's *déjà vu* all over again." This is one of my favorite Yogi-isms, which is the official term for off-the-wall quotes from legendary baseball hall-of-famer Yogi Berra. It's also redundant and unnecessary. I did it right there; I didn't need to say redundant *and* unnecessary; only one of the words is sufficient.

I suppose if you're writing poetry, you have an implicit right to exercise tautology to your heart's content. In areas where you have space to hammer home your meaning, feel free to employ tautology. I think that, in general, we have the poetic capacity of a haiku; every syllable and breath counts.

Maybe I'm beating a dead horse (a.k.a. committing idiomatic tautology) by writing an entire article on tautology. Perhaps I could have simply said, "Be brief and then be done." However, I felt it necessary to explore the proverbial halls of the City of Tautology City City Hall.

What in the word?

Cologne is a nice-smelling perfume.
A *colon* is either a punctuation mark (:)
or part of the large intestine.
It is not a good idea to comment on the smell
of someone's colon.
While I'm at it, I should point out that *bowl*
and *bowel* are different things as well.

Don't try too hard to be the cool boss

Slang is a language that rolls up its sleeves, spits on its hands and goes to work.
—Carl Sandburg

Let's face it: the trajectory of our language is trending slangular (a word I'm confident I just invented). With the proliferation and pervasiveness of internet culture, slang is everywhere. You know this is true when your grandma comments that your new shoes are *on fleek*. What is slang, and how should we properly utilize it in our communication?

If you're a boss, supervisor or even the Associate V.P. of Synergy, you don't need to be best buddies with your subordinates. Unfortunately, I disagree with Dunder Mifflin Scranton regional manager Michael Scott when he says, "I guess the atmosphere that I've tried to create here is that I'm a friend first and a boss second, and probably an entertainer third." You don't need to kowtow to the hipster youth culture by trying to speak their lingo. If you're trying too hard to incorporate slang that you can't pull off, it's only going to backfire; you'll be a fifty-something in skinny jeans complaining about the cost of avocado toast.

It's time to load up our slangshots to bring down the definition of slang. Slang is informal language spoken by a specific group of people. These words and phrases incubate among particular groups—whether they be teenagers, minority groups or certain geographical regions. Slang starts conversationally, whether or not it ever translates into written language. Using slang is a way for individuals to communicate with their own sets of words that help them to identify as part of a group.

Slang isn't jargon. Jargon is language that applies to a particular professional group. So, for instance, you'll hear tons of medical jargon in a TV hospital drama: "The patient has a localized, sub-therapeutic, idiopathic, epidermal pathogen that needs to be stabilized, stat!" To be honest, I have no idea what any of that means; however, since these seemingly foreign terms are specific to the medical community, they count as jargon, not slang.

Let's march through an incomplete recent history of slang with a few examples. In the '20s, if you called your sandwich the *bee's knees* or the *cat's pajamas*, you'd be saying that it was a particularly good sandwich. In the 1950s, if you had a shiner (black eye), you might want to cover it up with a pair of shades (sunglasses). In the 1960s, you'd be bummed out (depressed) if a choice babe (pretty girl) rejected your advances. If you're still telling people to *talk to the hand*, the 1990s called from their gigantic cell phone; they want back their slang term for a scornful rejection of what someone has said.

Use slang in informal situations: in conversations, at parties, online and when communicating with people with whom you already have a well-developed rapport. Don't use slang on your résumé, in a job interview, in a Nobel prize acceptance speech, or in any kind of formal writing, which includes business emails.

Although I'm a fan of slang, you need to exercise caution when using it, especially in writing; a misplaced use of *off the chain* in the wrong context will not only lose you style points, but it could also hurt your chances of getting ahead at work.

○ ○ ○ ○ ○

Start your own business

I like to start things. I've started at least six blogs in as many years. I've purchased at least a dozen website URLs in the past few years. How many have reached maturity?

Maybe one. Don't do as I do, but do as I say. Here's a business idea that's sure to make you the talk of your hipster neighborhood.

Let's face it: fancy toast is the new cupcake. My friend Melvin is thinking about opening an artisanal toast bar in SoNoHoBro, the hippest area of town that you haven't even heard of yet. If he wants to make some dough in this endeavor, Melvin can't just loaf around all day. And, if you ask me, this seems like as good a time as any to better understand direct and indirect objects.

As an aspiring new business owner, Melvin needs some money. So you might say something like "Melvin secured a loan from the bank." In this sentence, "Melvin" is the subject. The subject of a sentence is the noun that is doing or being something. A direct object is a noun that receives the action performed by the subject. What did Melvin secure? A loan. "Loan" is the direct object.

Suppose Melvin's toast bar, The Toast Office, is now celebrating its grand opening, and he's hired his brother Kelvin to be the senior jam spreader. While Mel thought it would be fitting to attempt the ceremonial ribbon cutting with a butter knife, it didn't work out well. As a result, Kelvin carefully handed the giant scissors to Melvin. In this sentence, "Kelvin" is the subject. "Scissors" is the direct object because it is the noun that receives Kelvin's action. "Melvin" is the indirect object. An indirect object (Melvin) is the recipient of the direct object (scissors).

A few weeks later, The Toast Office is the white-hot epicenter of SoNoHoBro's cultural scene. Mel and Kel have modified their toasters to make the springs superpowered, and the customers are encouraged to catch the toast on their plates (think Benihana, but with hot bread). The toaster propels the artisanal toast to the customer. In this sentence, the "toaster" (subject) propels the artisanal "toast" (direct object) to the "customer" (indirect object). I think we're getting the hang of it now.

In order to start a successful toast bar business, it's important to remember four things: put a hair net over your man bun, have a gluten-free option, always have an abundant stock of fresh avocados, and know your direct and indirect objects. Do these things and your trendy startup will be the toast of the town.

○ ○ ○ ○ ○

How to decide on the right name for your startup

You've got a killer idea for your new business. You found cheap office space in a reasonably safe part of town. You convinced your college roommate to work with you on your dream. Now all you have to do is name your company and watch the cash start flowing.

The problem is that most of the cool names are already taken. Not only that, but you want to be able to snag your domain name on the 'net. It's time to smoosh some words together with a fun grammar trick called bicapitalization (or BiCapitalization). Another name for this phenomenon is camel case, because the uppercase letter in the middle of a word looks like the hump of a camel.

I know what you're thinking, and—no—bicapitalization is not the thing where a guillotine cuts off two people's heads in one fell swoop. No, bicapitalization is when you capitalize another letter in the middle of a word. All the cool brands are doing it: YouTube, DreamWorks, eBay, SpaceX, and OkCupid. You can't throw a rock inside the world wide web without hitting a site whose company's name uses bicapitalization.

I don't go anywhere without my ChapStick. If I want a package to get somewhere fast, I'll drop it off at a FedEx store. I don't own a PlayStation, but it's another example of bicapitalization. Back in the late '90s, I enjoyed perusing MySpace and AltaVista. I love watching SportsCenter in the morning. You get the idea.

Steve Jobs toyed with bicapitalization for years. He famously placed the first online pizza order from his NeXT computer on a website called CyberSlice. When he reunited with Apple, Jobs later created the iMac, iPod, iPhone, iPad, and iEverythingElse. There's something edgy and non-conformist about bicapitalization that makes the concept irresistible to some tech brands.

So, here's my advice on naming your startup: take two words that relate to your product or idea and cram them together. Get rid of that space but retain the caps. Before you know it, you'll be the Founder and CEO of PumpkinPuppy, NachoPurse, GranolaJuice, or GlobePunt. At the time of this writing, all four of these .com domains are available. You can thank me later for the great idea.

○ ○ ○ ○ ○

A winning formula to size up any restaurant

I'm not a food critic, but I do know how to judge a restaurant accurately. Forget portion size, ambiance or availability of fresh, cage-free avocados; when I want to size up a restaurant, I head straight for the bathroom. If the bathroom has a Dyson Airblade hand dryer, it deserves at least two Michelin stars; if it has a regular hand dryer or (gasp) archaic paper towels made from tree meat, I have some serious doubts about the establishment. For the record, the Mitsubishi Electric Jet Towel dryer is an acceptable second place hand drying solution to the Dyson unit.

How do you judge a person's writing? We've all learned that we shouldn't judge a book by its cover (although a good cover really does help). In the same way I can tell a restaurant is going to be amazing based on its choice of hand dryers, I can tell someone's writing will be fantastic based on his use of semicolons.

What are semicolons? Think of them as super commas. They're the mutant offspring of a colon, a period and a comma. A semicolon's primary job is to connect two independent clauses that are related to the same idea in the same sentence. Here's an example:

> I'm thinking of buying a new superyacht; I spilled champagne on my old one and now it's sticky.

In this sentence, each clause before and after the semicolon can stand on its own as a complete sentence. However, they're linked by the same common idea, which is the purchase of a new superyacht. This is the main way to use a semicolon.

Like any superhero, it's cool to have more than one superpower. This is also true for our friend, the semicolon. You should also use a semicolon between items in a list or in a series if any of these items contain commas. For example:

> There are two types of people in this world: people who know how to use a semicolon, which makes them amazing and heroic; and people who won't get invited to my Oscars watch party, which will boast at least three chocolate fountains.

If your list or series doesn't include a comma, it doesn't need a semicolon.

Semicolons can do a masterful job of connecting ideas and clauses in your writing. Used properly and sparingly, they're like watching a bald eagle soaring over Mount Rushmore at dusk on the Fourth of July; however, if you overuse them, you're stuck with a restaurant full of fancy hand dryers and no food.

Instead of bringing coffee, just give people cash

Going on a coffee run for your coworkers sounds like a great idea, doesn't it? Not only do you seem considerate of their caffeine needs, but you also offer to pay (usually), which makes you seem generous. You're the hero of the office! But then you have to take down all their complicated orders, take the drinks away in one of those multi-cup holder things without spilling them all over your car (or your shirt), and then bring the correct drinks to everyone. Seems like a hassle, doesn't it? The next time you have this idea, just hand out five dollar bills instead.

Here's a free invention idea for you (as long as you name it after me): someone needs to invent a cup carrier that has built-in slots for seat belts. That way, you'd be able to secure your scalding cargo without ruining your interior. I call it "The Honeycutt Hot Holder Holster." I can almost see it on shelves in the "beyond" section at Bed Bath & Beyond.

Everyone wants to be the office hero, but not everyone knows the right time to use *bring* or *take*. The problem is, both words have similar meanings. Both words are verbs that involve carrying something, whether literally or figuratively. *Bring* means to carry something along with you while *take* means to carry something away with you.

For example, when the barista finishes making everyone's espresso drinks (quick tip: it's *espresso*, not *expresso*), you take the drinks from her. Similarly, you would bring the drinks to your coworkers. However, if I, as your boss, asked you to deliver coffee to the accounting department down the hall, I would say, "Please take this bucket of coffee to the accounting team."

It all comes down to the difference between *toward* and *away*. When the object is coming toward the person speaking, use *bring*. When the object is going away from the person speaking, use *take*. *Bring* indicates movement toward the writer/speaker, while *take* indicates movement away from the writer/speaker.

Take this advice to heart. Soon enough, your office mates will be bringing you piles of compliments on your journey up the corporate ladder.

○ ○ ○ ○ ○

Corporate synergy

Can something sound wrong, but actually be right? Take, for instance, French fries dipped in a Wendy's Frosty. This combination shouldn't be good, but it's actually a dollar menu match made in heaven. There's something indelibly delicious about the salty, slightly crispy potato strips when they fuse with the frozen soft-serve sweetness of the Frosty. Believe me, Wendy's isn't paying me as some kind of a grammar columnist/cultural influencer (although, I'd happily accept tall stacks of its fine Frosty money). Fries dipped in a Frosty sounds wrong, but it's so right.

What's the grammar equivalent of the Frosty-French fry connection? How about the word *gotten*? You probably use it and simultaneously think "wait, that can't be right, can it?" Let's explore.

I'll clear this up right away: British English doesn't use *gotten*; instead, it used *got* as the past participle of *get*. The British also call "French fries" "chips" and drive on the wrong side of the road. I suppose you can't be right all the time.

"What is a past participle?" some may ask. Let's have a quick refresher. A past participle is one of the four principle parts of a verb. It usually signifies an action that has been completed. With regular verbs, simply add *had, have* or *has* before the verb and *-ed* to the end to get your past participle. Examples include *have played, had closed* and *has purchased.* However, many verbs are irregular; *get* is one of these irregular verbs (and adding fiber to its diet hasn't changed a thing).

The present tense of *get* is *get*. *Get's* past tense is *got*. In American English, the past participle of *get* is *(have) gotten*. You would be correct to say, "I have gotten lazy in studying my Eastern European capitals lately." Consider another example: I have gotten many angry emails from red-pen-toting grammar purists lately. Even though it may sound wrong, it's technically correct grammar to use *gotten* with a companion word such as *have, has,* or *had*. That doesn't mean I like it.

No, I don't like *gotten*. Instead, I encourage you to use nicer-sounding words like *become* or *grown* in the first above example or *obtained* or *received* in the second example. The next time you read "Grammar Guy" in your favorite news-paper[1], I hope to write something like: This columnist has received a lifetime endorsement deal from Wendy's; after all, sometimes the most unlikely combinations turn out to be perfect partnerships.

○ ○ ○ ○ ○

A.C.R.O.N.Y.M.S.

I have some urgent news: there's an epidemic sweeping the country. So far, scientists haven't found a cure, but I'm happy to report that it's preventable. It leaves people looking foolish in front of other people they're trying to impress at parties and can, in rare cases, cause a breakup of a romantic rela-tionship. I'm talking about RAS Syndrome.

RAS Syndrome stands for Redundant Acronym Syn-drome...Syndrome. While everyone knows that saying *ATM*

---

1 If your newspaper doesn't carry my weekly column, drop everything and email, call, and write letters to your local paper's editor. Also, buy a subscription to your local paper.

machine is redundant, have you ever talked to someone about forgetting your *PIN number* every time you're at the ATM? *PIN* already stands for *Personal Identification Number*, so saying *PIN number* is redundant. You don't want to look like a doofus in front of your financial planner! He'll remove you from his preferred-monocle client list faster than you can say IRA account.

Does your new TV have an LCD display? Because that's redundant as well. So is saying *DC Comics*—*DC* already stands for *Detective Comics*, although the only situation in which you'd be shamed for that redundancy is probably the Comic-Con convention.

I can't tell you how many times I've heard this one: "Yeah, go ahead and send me that logo in a PDF format." *PDF* stands for *Portable Document Format*. The only thing that would make that more redundant would be if you said, "Please send that logo file over in a PDF format for Matt."

Although I'm sure you mean to be polite, writing *Please RSVP* on an invitation is technically redundant: *RSVP* is an abbreviation for the French expression *répondez s'il vous plaît*, which means *please respond*. Saying *Please RSVP* is the same as saying *Please, please respond*. After all, you don't want to sound desperate to get people to your fancy rooftop party.

I'm not sure if an entire sports team can contract RAS Syndrome, but, if it did, it would be the *LA Angels*. When translated into English, *Los Angeles* means *The Angels*. So, technically, *the LA Angels* is the same as saying *the The Angels Angels*.

Now for the lightning round. If you utter any of the following phrases, you've caught the RAS Syndrome: *ISBN number, UPC code, HIV virus, GOP party, SAT test, PAC committee, Gob Bluth, NPR radio, CSS sheet,* and *OPEC countries*. By preventing RAS Syndrome in your speech and correspondence, you'll avoid looking dumb in social, business, and romantic situations.

Don't be a jerk

Are you a snob, jerk, or both? When you wear your gold-rimmed monocle to the grocery store, it's a bit over the top. So, maybe you're a snob with jerk-like tendencies.

Are you a jerk or a snob when you judge someone who calls an initialism an acronym? Most people probably think they know what an acronym is, but let's review. An acronym is an abbreviation where the abbreviation is formed from letters of other words, usually the first letter of each word. This abbreviation (to be considered an acronym) needs to be pronounceable as its own word. Examples include *NASA* (National Aeronautics and Space Administration), *radar* (Radio Detection and Ranging), *SWAT* (Special Weapons and Tactics), and *taser* (Thomas A. Swift's Electric Rifle).

If you are pronouncing the abbreviation as its own word, your resulting word is an acronym. On the other hand, if you're pronouncing the letters of each word, you've got an initialism on your hands. Examples of initialisms include *DVD* (digital versatile disc), *FBI* (Federal Bureau of Investigation), and *FYI* (for your information). Initialisms are traditionally capitalized.

Now things get murky, thanks to the internet. Are internet slang abbreviations like *LOL* (laughing out loud) and *ROFL* (rolling on the floor laughing) acronyms or initialisms? I've heard people pronounce each of these abbreviated phrases using just the letters as wells as spoken phonetically. In the case of *ROFL*, the acronym version rhymes with *awful*. And, with the proliferation of texting and social media commenting, these abbreviations are increasingly not capitalized. In fact, if you capitalize them, you might be accused of being an old person.

As popular usage of the term *acronym* has expanded to include initialisms, I wouldn't be surprised if dictionaries follow suit to include initialisms in the definition of acronyms (much as *figuratively* has been added as a definition under *literally*). Does that make it right? Not necessarily. But, if you're going to correct people constantly about it, you'll probably be called both a snob and a jerk—even though you're right.

What in the word?

Stationary is when something is not moving.
Stationery is paper you write on to compose a letter.

Work no-no's

There's an old saying: two wrongs don't make a right. The idea is (for example) if your neighbor wrongs you by borrowing your hedge clippers and forgets to return them, it doesn't make things better to send a large, unwanted pizza delivery to his house so he has to pay for it. Those two negatives don't make a positive. Also, it kind of makes you a jerk.

In English, two negatives actually do make a positive. Most of the time people don't realize that using a double negative (also known as a negative concord) in a sentence implies the exact opposite of the speaker's intention, technically speaking.

For instance: *I don't got no time for that.* The person saying this probably means that she doesn't have time for whatever *that* is, but when she uses *don't* and *no* in the same sentence, these negative words cancel each other out to imply that the speaker does, in fact, have time for *that*. In the same way, saying "He's not going nowhere" implies that he is actually going somewhere. It's kind of confusing, and, to be quite honest, it's bad grammar. A nice way of saying this is the usage of double negatives in speech or writing is broadly considered nonstandard English.

Now it's time to introduce some complicating factors into the mix (as when, for instance, your neighbor spots you hiding in the bushes and spying on him while he deals with the unwanted pizza delivery). In many other languages (including Portuguese, Russian, Spanish, Italian and Polish) double negatives are commonly used to intensify the implied negation. The two negatives create a snowball effect in the sentence, creating an emphatic, super negative.

Not only that, but certain dialects of American English employ double negatives in their vernacular to the same effect as the foreign languages I listed above. I suppose if you're with a group of people who all understand what you mean when you use a double negative, then it's acceptable, similar to special house rules in poker. However, in more formal settings, double negatives should be avoided. When it comes to more buttoned-up situations (especially in important scenarios like job interviews and reciting wedding vows), you should avoid double negatives. After all, I think we could all benefit from a healthy dose of positivity.

○ ○ ○ ○ ○

Getting lit at company events

I'm a lamp guy. I love lamps. I'm not just saying that because I'm naming things I see in the room; lamps serve a functional purpose and provide beauty in a room. So when I see a great lamp at an antique store or at an upscale garage sale, you'd better believe I'm going to buy it, put it in the backseat and put a seatbelt on it.

But the real question is, once I find the right spot in my living room for my new lamp, does it make the area *well-lit* or *well-lighted*? What is the difference between *lit* and *lighted*? I'm on the case.

The super-short answer is both *lit* and *lighted* are correct past tense forms of light. Technically, *lit* is considered an irregular verb because you have to change the spelling of light to make it past tense, whereas *lighted* is regular because you simply add -*ed*. While over the years, *lit* has gained popularity in common usage, there are some distinct ways each word predominantly gets used.

Lit is usually used as the simple past tense verb of *light*. It means to illuminate or set on fire.

> After we lit Aunt Helen's birthday candles, her hair inadvertently caught on fire when she got too close to the cake.

> The fireflies' pleasantly blinking butt muscles lit the dark forest clearing.

Lighted can either be used as an adjective or a past tense verb. When *lighted* is used as an adjective, it's synonymous with *being illuminated*:

> The brightly lighted living room shone brilliantly thanks to dad's new leg lamp.

> The glow of my lighted torch allowed us to see in the secret cave.

As a past tense verb, *lighted* should be used as the past participle of *light*. As a reminder, a past participle verb usually requires an auxiliary word in front of it, like *had* or *have*:

> We had already lighted our glowsticks by the time the dance party got into full swing.

Although *lit* and *lighted* are technically interchangeable (and therefore correct), in popular usage, *lit* is more commonly used in the simple past tense while *lighted* is more commonly used as a past participle verb.

Happy lamp shopping. Just don't get too lit or you'll end up with the lampshade on your head.

What in the word?

Inflammable means that something is burnable.
This doesn't make sense, but it is true.
Flammable also means that something is burnable.
Go figure.
Nonflammable means that something is not burnable.

Don't trust autocorrect when texting your boss

For once it's not the millennials getting the blame for the downfall of civilization. Right now, I'm blaming Apple. But the good news is, if anyone from Apple is reading this book (I've heard grammar books are big in Cupertino), they can fix this with a quick update to their iOS.

Recently, one of Apple's autocorrect features had a hiccup: when people typed in *I* it would autocorrect to *A*. A couldn't believe what A was seeing. Fortunately, enough people brought it to Apple's attention that the company that gave birth to Siri (or was it the other way around?) fixed the bug in an iOS update.

As an iPhone user, I can't speak for Android or Windows-based phones, but Apple's autocorrect gets confused when I type plural days of the week. Sometimes it adds an unnecessary apostrophe and sometimes it leaves Tuesdays alone. And, remember my apostrophe philosophy: apostrophes are like sentence confetti, adding a fun flair to your scintillating syntax. But a misplaced apostrophe is like confetti at a funeral: inappropriate and impossible to undo.

When I type "I like to eat waffles on Fridays" into a text message, Apple's iOS correctly leaves my sentence alone. However, when I thumb-type "I hate Mondays almost as much as Garfield," autocorrect changes *Mondays* to *Monday's*. In this instance, "Mondays" doesn't have ownership of anything, so what gives?

The tricky thing is, texting "Did you see last Monday's episode of *The Bachelor*?" is correct, but "On Mondays, I watch *The Bachelor* with my trusty box of Franzia" is also correct. And my autocorrect leaves both alone. In the first example, the episode aired on Monday, so "Monday's" is correct. In the second example, I'm talking about something I do on Mondays; nothing belongs to Monday in this sentence.

So it seems when you type pluralized days of the week on their own (i.e., I hate Mondays), Apple's autocorrect incorrectly apostrophizes my texts.[2] Can someone call or text Apple and let them know? Let's harness the power of the written word to address an incredibly minor (but kind of annoying) grammar glitch.

○ ○ ○ ○ ○

Sending heated emails

I truly believe good grammar can make your life more awesome. It can lead to job opportunities, romantic relationships and even a syndicated column that makes you hyper-specifically famous. Perhaps one day you'll even write a book that tens of people purchase and read. Conversely, bad grammar can turn your life into a country song. You can lose your job, your truck, your honey and your dog if your grasp of language suffers. That's not entirely true; your dog will always forgive you.

---

2 Apostrophize is a real word, my friend.

I want to encourage you to read your emails twice before sending them. I'll go one step further and say the same rule applies to tweets and Facebook posts. Fairly or not, people make judgments about you based on the level of correctness of your syntax.

The other day I received a hilariously ironic email that decried the state of grammar among our nation's youths. The writer passionately went on for a page-length paragraph about how our collective grammar is going down the drain. She had some fair points; however, the subject line of her email was "Grammer Guy." That's my other newspaper column.

"Grammer Guy" is a column dedicated to the acting brilliance and smooth baritone voice of Kelsey Grammer. Did you know he received Emmy nominations while on three different television series for portraying Frasier Crane? Personally, I prefer his work as the voice of Sideshow Bob in *The Simpsons*.

Okay, so "Grammer Guy" isn't a thing. Although, if enough people respond positively to this idea, I just may have to write about it. I only point out the irony of a gaffe like "Grammer Guy" because the lady who sent me the email was railing against the state of our careless and un-informed grammar.

There are a few easy ways to avoid spelling and grammar gaffes in your public communications. First, read your work aloud prior to sending it. You'll catch at least half of your errors merely by reading to yourself. Secondly, get another set of eyes on your writing before hitting the send button. The need for a proofreader increases in direct proportion to your level of fervor; if you're fired up, have someone you trust read over your shoulder before you put your two cents out in the world. Double check your grammar before laying down the hammer.

Lying will likely get you in trouble

Sure, it's easy to distinguish *lace* from *lice* and *lake* from *like*, but what's the difference between *lay* and *lie*? When I say "lie" in this essay, I'm not referring to the act that causes Pinocchio's nose to grow; I'm talking about the occasion when someone reclines.

The quick answer to this confusing conundrum is this: *lay* requires a direct object while *lie* does not. You lie down in the fetal position sucking your thumb when you're super-stressed watching a Colts game. You lay down a brass unicorn paperweight on important papers so your office's industrial strength air conditioner doesn't whoosh them away and risk paper cutting your entire department.

Allow me to lay down a few examples:

> King Lear lays his lyre down on the linoleum landing of his lopsided lake lair.

In this case, "lyre" is the direct object, so "lay" is correct.

> Lance lies lazily in his limo, lunching on Lay's and listening to Lyle Lovett's lavish lyrics.

Lance lies down on his own, while Lear lays the direct object (his lyre) down.

Now it gets complicated; the past tense of *lie* is *lay*, while the past tense of *lay* is *laid*. So, you could correctly say:

> John Lennon lay down on the floor while he laid down the lead vocal track to "Revolution 1."

The English language strikes again.

> While on vacation in Hawaii, Linus laid a lei on Elaine while she lay on the beach.

> You can lie about laying down your laser while you lie on the loveseat in your lounge.

It's a wonder anyone learns to speak English as a second language. We often assume and expect others to possess a mastery of the English language while its rules are ridiculously complicated and, once you think you understand it, someone comes along with a half dozen head-scratching exceptions.

To take a *Hamilton* quote out of context, sometimes I feel English is "such a blunder, sometimes it makes me wonder why I even bring the thunder." Yet our language's seemingly contradictory rules awaken our inner word nerds and cause us to lie in bed while we dream about the truth.

○ ○ ○ ○ ○

How to avoid looking like a dinosaur in your emails and T.P.S. reports

How many spaces should go after a period: one or two? To answer that question, we have to talk about typewriters.

A long time ago in a galaxy far, far away, people learned to type on manual typewriters. If this describes you, you likely learned to add two spaces after a period. That's because manual typewriters used monospaced type, in which each character takes up the same amount of horizontal space. Adding two spaces after a period while typing on a manual typewriter allowed for better readability.

Most fonts on computers utilize what's called proportional type. This means skinny letters like *i* and *l* are closer to each other, as opposed to wider letters like *w* and *m*. So, unless you're a hipster who is ironically using a typewriter in a public place, use only one space after the end of a sentence.

Does it matter? Great question. If the argument for double spacing is readability, then in the case of our modern computer fonts, which use proportional spacing, you do not need two spaces. Proportional fonts don't have unnecessary space, so two spaces are redundant. If you use two spaces, you might be giving the impression that technology warped off into hyperspeed while you missed the ship because you stayed to hear the end of the cantina band's interstellar set.

Back in high school, I chose Courier New (a mono-spaced font) to type papers in my English class. This took a 3 ½ page paper (on a book I skimmed, at best) in Times New Roman or Arial (which are proportional fonts) and stretched into a 5-pager. I'm sure my English teacher rolled her eyes when she saw all the extra space, however it did allow her extra room to write things like "next time, try harder" and "disappointing!" in the margins.

If you instinctively tap the spacebar twice after the end of a sentence, you have two options: either employ the find-and-replace feature in your word processing software to replace all instances of two spaces with one space (Google it—it's pretty easy). Option two is to train yourself to slice your spaces in half with your glowing laser sword as if the galaxy depends on it. May the space be with you.

What in the word?

To *flesh out* something is to build on an idea
to make it viable.
To *flush out* something is to make something
leave its hiding place.

How not to get hired using social media

Did you know that most prospective employers check your social media account as an unofficial step in the job interview process? Yikes. That means they probably scrolled through to see your late night, all caps rant about whichever political party you oppose, as well as your *Bachelorette* finale live-tweeting session (I can't believe Gwenifer picked him either, you guys!). The same goes for basic grammar and spelling. It's time to tackle three Facebook foibles and Twitter trip-ups that may prevent you from getting hired for the job you want.

If you're looking for a great job, you need to know your grammar. Did you catch what I did there? Too often I see people use *your* when they should use *you're*. *Your* is something you own or possess; *you're* is the contraction (or mash up, as I like to call it) of *you* and *are*. Believe it or not, using these two words incorrectly makes Clippy the Microsoft Word assistant weep himself rusty.

When you write "I hope the Colts don't lose again," you likely hope they score more points than the Patriots. When you write "I hope the Colts don't loose again," you're suggesting they remember to put on their belts so their pants don't fall down. See the difference?

There names a place, thing or the existence of something: I think I left my chapstick over there. To check if you're using *there* correctly, see if you can replace *there* with *here*.

Their shows possession:

> I can't believe those chowder-eating cheaters the Patriots deflated their footballs.

To check if you're using *their* correctly, see if you can replace *their* with *our*.

They're is a *mash up* of *they* and *are*:

Huzzah, they're having a sale on Burt's Bees lip balm at Target!

To check if you're using *they're* correctly, see if you can replace *they're* with *they are.*

Yes, in addition to the topics of your social media posts, employers also look at the content of your character count. So, what's the lesson here? Treat every post as if your future HR director is watching; practice common sense in your spelling and your socializing.

○ ○ ○ ○ ○

How not to get your sandwich stolen

When it comes to writing, you should always use active voice. You should utilize active voice as often as possible so those reading your prose will understand perfectly and clearly what you're trying to say. In active voice writing, the subject of the sentence does the action:

The unicorn (subject) started (verb) a game of hide-and-seek over 4,000 years ago; he's still hiding.

My coworker (subject) threw (verb) a fit after I submerged his stapler in Jell-O.

This straightforward approach keeps your sentences from being too complicated.

When it comes to writing, you should always avoid passive voice. Passive voice creeps in unexpectedly if you aren't careful. This happens when your subject no longer does the action in the sentence. Instead, your subject is being acted on by the verb. In these sentences, the subject usually comes after the verb:

A game of hide-and-seek was started by the unicorn over 4,000 years ago; he's still hiding.

A fit was thrown by my coworker after I submerged his stapler in Jell-O.

See the difference?

Some telltale signs of sentences using passive voice include the following words and phrases: was, were, has been, have been, are and is, to name a few. Sometimes you just can't avoid passive voice, but when you can, do it; your writing will jump off the page.

In general, you should avoid passive-aggressive voice. I think this is more important than avoiding passive voice. I'll provide some examples:

The unicorn's friends, instead of telling him his breath smelled like rotten mermaid eggs, opted to run away from him during a game of hide-and-seek.

Because I disagreed with my co-worker's promotion, I decided to secretly submerge his stapler in Jell-O.

While active voice leaves your reader with a sense of purpose and action, passive voice seems anemic and unsure of itself. Passive-aggressive voice, on the other hand, will simply cause your friends, roommates and coworkers to stop inviting you to parties offering free cake. Choose your path wisely.

Win at Life

How good grammar will help you achieve your wildest dreams

This section is all about how to achieve massive success at life in general. For instance, you should be rooting for the Detroit Lions professional American football team, and you should steer away from preferring the Washington Redskins. According to a Wall Street Journal/Grammarly study, Redskins fans' comments on the team's website had the worst spelling, punctuation and grammar compared to comments on other team sites. Lions fans had the lowest percentage of phonetic foibles, making the Detroit fanbase the most astute at the English language. Whether or not you love a team who plays on turf in a domed stadium, you can't argue with the numbers. These numbers, unfortunately for Lions fans, do not factor into playoff considerations.

For those of you who love grammar but don't know much about competitive sports ball, allow me to give you a quick tip on how to participate in conversations about the local sports team in a way that makes you seem like you know what you're talking about. Whether you're at the coffee shop, the local watering hole or at a weekly meeting of your area tandem bicycle club, simply start the conversation by saying, "Can you believe that game last night?! Man, it was some game!"

Assuming the other person is a fan of your regional team, they'll probably take the conversation from there, going on and on about the clutch drive that either won or lost the contest. Your introductory statements regarding the team's performance cover you in the case of a win, loss or tie. And, if the other person isn't a fan of sports-watching, they're likely to agree with you and change the subject to the economy or something like that.

Good grammar plays a crucial albeit largely invisible role in your overall success and well-being. By mastering the following tips, people will wonder aloud what your secret sauce is after you leave the room. *Does Carla do yoga? What does she eat for breakfast? I heard she doesn't even own a TV. Do you think fish oil makes her so remarkable as a human being? I heard fish oil is supposed to be good for you.* Your acquaintances will only be able to form their own hypotheses on what makes you a capital *W* "Winner." Maybe she's born with it; maybe it's good grammar.

○ ○ ○ ○ ○

Setting a good New Years' resolution (or New Years' revolution)

Since Julius Caesar proposed the aptly named Julian calendar in 45 B.C.E., people have been making bold resolutions to improve themselves. For the record, Caesar's resolution didn't work that year, as his best friend literally stabbed him in the back the following year. This arbitrary turning of a new calendar page gives us a sense that *this year things can be different.* Possibilities abound—until you start comparing yourself to other people.

If you go to the gym in January, for example, it's not fair to compare yourself to the guy who is bench pressing a Volkswagen in front of the mirror; he's stronger than you. Of course, going to the gym leads me to think of grammar questions, such as when do you add *-er* to a comparative adjective and when do you add *more* in front of it? There should be rules about these things.

Fortunately for us, there are rules on comparative adjective construction! For adjectives with just one syllable (like "strong" in the example), simply add *-er* to the end of the word. In the case of two-syllable adjectives that do not end in *-y* (and for all adjectives with three or more syllables), add *more* before the word. Examples include *more generous* and *more intelligent*. When two-syllable adjectives end in *-y,* change the *y* to an *i* and add *-er*; this is the case in words such as *skinnier* and *happier*.

When you compare three or more things, you move from the realm of the comparative into superlative territory. "I was the weakest person in the entire weight room," you might write in your exercise journal. With one-syllable adjectives, simply add *-est* to make an adjective superlative. If the adjective already ends in *e*, simply add *-st*. For short words that follow the consonant-vowel-consonant pattern, double the last consonant before adding *-est*. For example:

> My wallet wasn't the fattest in the country club, but it also wasn't the thinnest.

For two-syllable adjectives ending in *y*, also add *-est* to form the superlative. For most other two-syllable adjectives, add the word *more* before the adjective:

> I had the happiest, most peaceful start to my year!

For most three or more syllable adjectives, use the *most* construction.

Whew, I'm out of shape on my grammar rules. I resolve to get faster, better and stronger when it comes to my grammar game.

The gym in January has got to be the worst place you can ever go. It's as if they were giving away free pizza or something. I avoid the gym in January for two reasons:

1. I enjoy paying the gym and in return I don't have to go there.

2. I generally don't like being around people all that much.

So I usually wait until early February to make my annual appearance at the gym. And when I do, there are reporters there waiting to find out if I see my shadow or not. "He saw his shadow; that means six more weeks of pretty much the same thing."

When I go to the gym, I set reasonably low expectations for myself. My goal at the gym is just to break even. So, I still get to eat pizza and ice cream whenever I want and I try to get back to even at the gym. I like to try out the weight machines, but I usually have to stalk someone beforehand so I know what I'm supposed to do. "Oh...you do that with your arms. I was going to try and karate kick it." And since my expectations are low, I have no problem with changing the amount of weight from the last guy. What is he, a professional weight lifter? He had this set at 120...I'll give 70 a try...or maybe 65. 60. Okay, 40. That's more like it. I'm going to do five sets of ten of these...or one set of six. Okay, great workout. I wonder if Papa John's delivers here?

January is resolution time, which means your local gym's treadmills will be in high demand while they glisten with other people's sweat (until roughly the end of February). You've probably set some goals for yourself and defined ways you'd like to be more awesome. Allow me to suggest an additional resolution: to win at life with better grammar.

We can start right now. Since January is the time to "lead off" a new year, let's examine the words *lead* and *led*, which often trip us up (just like that treadmill you set at a slightly-too-ambitious speed).

Lead is an example of a heteronym. Heteronyms are homographs that are spelled the same, have different meanings and sound different. *Lead* is not only a heavy metal with a short *e* vowel sound, but it is also when someone is in charge, or ahead of something (as a verb) or a position of advantage in a competition (as a noun), and has a long *e* vowel sound.

Use *led* as the past tense for the verb *lead* (the one that rhymes with bead):

> When you were in first place, you were in the lead; you led the race for 19 laps.

The confusion, of course, is when *lead* (like the metal) and *led* (the past tense verb) go head-to-head. These words are homophones, which are homonyms (words that sound the same) with different spellings. Homophones trick us, like the small print in the gym membership stating we can, under no circumstance, quit the gym.

This paragraph is a lightning round to clear up any other *lead/led* related words. *Leed* (with a long *e* vowel sound) is a Scottish word for language or speech. Led Zeppelin (with a short *e* vowel sound) was an English rock band, who, ironically, was one of the pioneering bands in the genre of heavy metal music (not pioneers in lead, the literal heavy metal). One of their favorite venues was Leeds University (pronounced with a long *e* vowel sound).

So, if you'd like to get the lead out when the new year rolls around, I suggest you lead the way by working out with Led Zeppelin blaring in your earbuds. And wipe down the treadmill before you use it.

◯ ◯ ◯ ◯ ◯

Some tips on adulting

I need to go to the dentist. I got my six-month appointment reminder a few months ago and promptly canceled.

"Would you like to reschedule?" asked the receptionist.

"No," I replied. "I'll get back to you."

It's not that I wanted to quit the dentist or anything, but balancing a new job, young kids and house maintenance is tough work. Adulting is hard.

Over the past ten years, the word "adult" has been verbified. And, before you blame the hypothetical 26-year-old self-described "emerging adult" who lives in his parents' basement, you have to consider the parents' role in all of this. Parents of millennials have practically turned coddling into a competitive sport. I'm not surprised that 24% of 25 to 34-year-olds in the U.S. now live at home.

Adulting (which shouldn't be used as a serious word) means to engage in adult-like behavior or activities. These things include (but are certainly not limited to) ironing your clothes, going to the dentist, eating vegetables and paying for your own insurance (instead of staying on mom and dad's plan).

After my freshman year of college while I was away at a summer internship, my parents actually sold my bed in a not-so-subtle way of telling me it was time to move out; I'm thankful they did.

Depending on its usage, *adulting* can be used jokingly by well-adjusted people in their twenties or thirties to refer to mundane daily tasks associated with normal life. Alternately, the term gets used unironically by (technically) adults who are waiting for someone to come and hand them their dream job.

Don't blame the economy. If you can't find a job, make one. Sorry to bring the Dr. Phil tough love here, but it's time to get out of the sweatpants and Crocs and create the opportunity you're waiting for.

You can adult. I believe in you. If you're a parent whose

man-child needs to read this, set it on his clothes you set out for him this morning. Do this only after you have read it yourself. It's time to empower people who are living in a constant state of *adultolescence* instead of holding them back by enabling their kid tendencies. Maybe then we can stop using *adult* as a verb and start actually being adults.

○ ○ ○ ○ ○

How to be a winner at the grocery store

If there's one subject I love, it's grammar rules. If there's one thing I know, it's grammar rules!

See what I did there? Now it's time to tackle a widespread grammar debacle currently plaguing the English-speaking world at an alarming pace. When should you say *less* and when should you say *fewer*? You've probably heard to use *less* for things you don't count and *fewer* for things you do count. As a general rule, this is true, but sooner than later you'll run into a slew of exceptions.

Instead, think about it this way: use *less* for something singular and *fewer* for something plural. For example:

I noticed less pulp in this orange juice this morning.

You could also say:

I found 55 fewer palpable pulp particles in this orange juice this morning.

On its own, "pulp" is singular, so less is correct. Because you have plural pulp particles, "fewer" is correct.

Here's where it gets tricky: when referring to time, distance or money, use *less* because we think of these types of things as singular amounts. For example:

The distance from Earth to the moon is (on average) 238,855 miles.

You wouldn't say "the distance from Earth to the moon are 238,855 miles." So, when you apply the singular or plural rule here, you could correctly say:

This rocket we built in our garage is really fast; we're already less than 100 miles away from the moon!

Now, what about the express lane at the grocery store? Is "10 items or less" correct, or should it be "10 items or fewer?" Although technically it should be "10 items or fewer," many argue that if a rule makes a phrase or sentence too cumbersome, drop it. I have a hard time declaring my allegiance to either side, so I'm going to offer a third option: up to 10 items. This way, grammar grouches don't get all grumpy and people who don't care never cared in the first place. Just as long as people don't try to sneak 13 bottles of pulpy orange juice into the express lane.

What in the word?

A *carrot* is a root vegetable that ruins cake.
A *karat* is a measurement of purity (e.g., 24 karat gold).
A *carat* is a unit of weight for diamonds and other precious gemstones.
A *caret* is a proofreading mark (^) that shows where something should be inserted into a document.

The invisible letter lurking at the end of the grocery store

I've lived in Indiana for twelve years now, and, prior to that, I was born and raised in Oklahoma. In both places, I couldn't help but notice the same strange phenomenon when people talked about shopping at grocery stores. For some reason, people tend to add an *s* to the end of the name of the store.

In the Midwest, I hear Aldi's, Meijer's, and Kroger's all the time. In Oklahoma, I heard several people say Wal-Mart's. I don't think people are suggesting they went to multiple Kroger stores, so that's why I wrote them as possessives instead of as plurals. Why do people do this?

It could be because some grocery stores already end in *s*, whether it's a possessive or plural name: *Whole Foods, Albertsons* (which used to be possessive, but now it's not), *Trader Joe's, Sprouts Farmers Market* (no apostrophe necessary), *Publix*, and—my favorite—*Schnucks*. Schnucks, a St. Louis-based regional chain, just sounds like a word you'd call someone if you wanted to characterize him as some sort of dense nincompoop.

On the other hand, some of these stores have their origins as possessive names. For instance, Meijer began as *Meijer's Thrifty Acres*, although Kroger started as *Kroger Grocery and Baking Company*. Did you know Wal-Mart was originally called *Walton's Five and Dime*? However, we don't call Wal-Mart *Walton's*, so why the *s* on the end of Wal-Mart? Sam's Club (founded by Wal-Mart founder Sam Walton) is like if Wal-Mart (which is already humongous) got exponentially bulkier, but I can't get in because they keep denying me a membership.

My guess is adding an *s* to the end of grocery store names is a holdover from when many stores used the last name of the store owners as their names. These "last name-apostrophe *s*" stores were so common that many people instinctively add an *s* to the end of the grocery store name, regardless of its name or origin.

As Aldi makes headlines as the fastest-growing grocery store chain in the U.S., expect to hear more people say "They're putting in a new Aldi's down the road." And Amazon purchased Whole Foods Market, but I don't expect to hear anyone saying "I get my groceries from Amazon's" anytime soon; if he did, he'd sound like a giant Schnuck.

○ ○ ○ ○ ○

Tots and bots: two things that make everyone's lives better

I need a Roomba. Okay, maybe "need" is a strong word, but...

...I need a Roomba. I just crunched the numbers, and getting a Roomba to robotically clean my floors would make my life approximately 4.5% better. Feel free to disagree with me, but Rosie (I just named my Roomba Rosie) will increase my quality of life. If anyone is wondering what to buy me for Christmas this year, now you know.

Feel free to disagree with me on this as well: parentheses make writing stronger. It's okay if you don't agree with my stance because—after all—everyone has their faults. Let's examine some rules on using parentheses accurately.

Parentheses block off information that either clarifies your writing or is used as an aside. To use parentheses to clarify the contents of your sentence, you could write: Americans consume 70 million pounds of tater tots per year (or the equivalent of 5 Eiffel Towers). Here's an example of how to use parentheses as an aside:

> Tater tots (or, as I like to call them, potato toddlers) are the best food in the world.

If your parenthetical clause ends your sentence, insert the period after your parentheses (not before). In fact, I just illustrated the point. To take things to the next level (like dipping your tots in sriracha ketchup), let's discuss punctuation inside your parentheses. If the contents of your parenthetical clause form a complete sentence, add punctuation!

> The brand name Tater Tots is trademarked by Ore-Ida (They were "invented" in 1953 by Ore-Ida co-founders F. Nephi and Golden Grigg.).

That being said, you can certainly overuse parentheses in your writing. This would be like running your Roomba all day, every day; instead of enhancing your life, it would just get in the way.

> If my Roomba sucked up the tater tots I left on the floor (I promise I was going to eat them later.), I'd have to sternly (in binary language, of course) reprimand her.

This over-utilization of parentheses gets in the way of an already interesting sentence. And—just like your relationship with your robot vacuum—never let parentheses (or tater tots) get in the way of a good thing.

○ ○ ○ ○ ○

The prime time to upgrade your van

It stinks getting tripped up by words, especially words that are practically identical. It's like trying to distinguish between a set of twins who look exactly the same except that one of them has a birthmark on the underside of his right pinky toe. This seems to be the case with long-lost word siblings *then* and *than*.

An easy way to remember when it's appropriate to use then is: *then* = *when*. As a general rule, you can use *then* as an adverb or an adjective with any sentence that has to do with time, what comes next, or what used to be. For instance, use *then* to replace *at that time*:

> I called you five minutes ago. Were you asleep then?

In addition, use *then* to imply the next in time, space or order:

> First we will eat tacos and then we'll dance in the fountain.

Then can also be a substitute for words like *accordingly* or *in that case*:

> If you provoke that angry jellyfish, then you will probably get stung.

Remember, *then* = *when*.

Although *than* looks eerily similar to *then,* its purpose is different. If *then* = *when*, then *than* = *van*. Allow me to explain: do you or does someone you know own a minivan? I can't tell you how many times I've seen a van owner inspect someone else's van in order to compare each other's vans. For example:

> Wow, Dave, your van has dual DVD players in the back seat; your van is way cooler than mine.

Than is used as a conjunction any time you're making a comparison, as van owners often do:

> You didn't get the heated leather seats? Mine is clearly better than yours.

Remember, *than* = *van*.

Let's put it all together in order to help you determine the most opportune time to acquire a new minivan:

> If you want to have a fancier van than Dan's, then you should probably buy the one with satellite WiFi.

What in the word?

Elude means to escape from something.
Allude means to make an indirect reference to something.

Stop apologizing for your dirty car.

> *Substitute "damn" every time you're inclined to write*
> *"very"; your editor will delete it and the writing will be*
> *just as it should be.*
> —Mark Twain

Here's the scene: you offer to drive to lunch, and, just before everyone gets in, you make a mad sweep around your car, grabbing old to-go cups and discarded wrappers and putting them in an old Wendy's bag. Maybe that's not you; perhaps your car is somewhat tidier. Regardless, just as everyone gets into your car, you commence with the obligatory statement that goes something like this: "Sorry, my car is such a mess. It's very dirty. I've been meaning to vacuum it out for the past six years."

Whether our car interiors are clean or not, we all repeat a version of the obligatory apology when we give someone else a ride. Guess what? It's unnecessary. You have permission to quit apologizing.

Here's a word we don't need to say anymore: *very.*

The book was very funny.

The Olympian jumped very high.

The president was very upset.

Yawn.

If *very* is overused as I suggest, what alternatives do we have? Let me propose two options. First, simply omit the word and proceed with your sentence as usual. As Mr. Twain suggests, you should simply search your entire document (when writing) or somehow audit your brain for words it knows (when speaking), then merely delete the word from your entire lexicon. You don't need to say or write *very* if you're using it as a *filler* or *padding* word. The same thing goes for the word *really*. Really.

You may still wish to convey the same kind of emphasis you think *very* injects. After all, *very* is an intensifier, which is an example of an adverb or adverbial phrase that shows emphasis, thereby making a phrase or sentence stronger. Very well; you can substitute scores of more interesting words for *very,* depending on the level of severity you'd like to communicate.

Rather than saying something is *very fast,* say it was *quick.* If you want to convey that something is *very good,* instead say that it is *superb.* Don't say *very hungry*; *ravenous* is much more interesting.

It may take more creativity, but substituting other words for *very* will infuse your speech with the exact intensity or tone you want. So either stop saying *very* or find a better word. Just as with the obligatory car apology, *very* is overused and often superfluous.

○ ○ ○ ○ ○

Celebrate Fall/Autumn properly

Call me *basic,* but I love fall. I have an extensive jacket wardrobe. I love pumpkin-flavored things. I love football season. I love raking leaves (for the first five minutes). I enjoy carving pumpkins with my family. Man, all this talk about fall and seasons makes me want to tackle when to capitalize seasons. Since I'm the one writing this book, I think I'll do just that.

What can I say? I'm on a capitalization kick lately. It's probably because I've been reading a book about George Washington featuring several examples of his correspondence. Those Founding Fathers loved capitalizing anything they deemed important (solemn abstractions like Life, Liberty and Happiness) and pretty much anything else they wanted to emphasize. I like their epistolary style.

First, let's look at correct usage when not capitalizing seasons. The basic rule is: do not capitalize seasons when you are using them generically. Here's an example:

> Indiana's humidity levels in the summer are off the charts.

And another:

> In Narnia, it is always winter, never Christmas.

Now, when should you upgrade seasons to proper noun status? When seasons are part of a proper noun, capitalize them. For example:

> Now that the Winter Olympics are over, I don't know what to do with myself.

And another:

> During Fall Semester 2005, I had a mystery virus that stumped all the doctors on campus. Eventually, my body fought it off and I survived.

Finally, let's examine *fall* and *autumn*—which is it? Do we need two words for the same thing? I like *fall* because it says what it is; not only do the leaves start to fall, but the temperatures do as well. In fact, spring and fall both appeared in English in the 16th century as "spring of the leaf" and "fall of the leaf." They were eventually shortened to *spring* and *fall.*

Autumn came from the French word *automne.* At this point, fall and autumn are interchangeable. I prefer *fall,* but won't judge anyone who uses *autumn,* although autumn is rather like fall's snooty cousin. I do think it's silly that we have two words that mean literally the same thing.

○ ○ ○ ○ ○

A confession about my 29th great-grandfather

What is a *relative?* Really, relations are all *relative,* so don't judge me if I tell you I come from royalty. I'll get to that in a second.

Does it bother anyone else that the word *subtle* has a silent *b?* Is it ironic that the word subtle means "understated?" The *b* in *subtle* is, therefore, itself, subtle. Are you with me?

We don't spell *settle* with a *b.* It's the same with *sidle, saddle,* and *Seattle.* There aren't *b's* in those words. So why the *b, subtle?*

Subtle started out its life as the Latin word *subtilis,* which was an adjective describing the thin, delicate material used for producing a veil. *Subtilis* hopped on a boat to France and became *soutil* in Old French. *Soutil* meant thin and delicate. Once William the Conqueror (my 29th great-grandfather on my mom's side) and the Normans invaded England in 1066, *soutil* made the journey across the English Channel as well, becoming *sotil* in Middle English. Its meaning grew beyond physical delicacy into the way we now understand *subtle* in an abstract way.

So what happened? Doesn't it make sense to drop letters that aren't pronounced in a word?

In the 17th century, a group of nerdy Englishmen, who were known as the Latinists[1], started respelling English words to ground them in their Latin origins (I think their mantra was

---

1   Another great potential band name.

"Make English Latin Again"). Because of this, they added *b's*, *l's*, and *p's* back into words that had evolved from Latin. *Sotil*, therefore, got its *b* added back into it, and it began to be spelled *subtle*. The *b*, however, stayed silent—subtle, even.

At this same time, several other words that started as Latin words ultimately arrived in our modern English lexicon with added letters in them. They, too, originated in Latin, then migrated into Old French, and rode the Norman wave into Middle English. These words include: *aisle, debt, doubt, indict, salmon, plumber* and *receipt*.

Some words, on the other hand, didn't lose their *b's*, even though the *b's* were no longer pronounced. They include *bomb* and *dumb*. That seems pretty dumb, if you ask me. And, while this is frustrating, it's only one of the myriad of complex historical reasons why English spelling is complicated and annoying. So, beware of falling under the spell of an unexpected *b*; you might just get stung by it.

○ ○ ○ ○ ○

Let the Brits have their tea: 'Merican grammar

"England and America are two countries separated by a common language."
—*George Bernard Shaw*

Right now we're trying to teach our daughter to crawl. She's eight months old, and I can only imagine how ridiculous I look down on the floor attempting to show her how to push her body up off the floor and start moving toward me. Or is it *towards* me? Is it *toward* or *towards*?

The more I look at *toward* and *towards*, the more I'm convinced neither of them is a real word. I think pretty much any word will do that to you. And shouldn't *toward* and *coward* rhyme? I'm too scared to look into it; I think that makes me a toward coward.

It really all depends on where you live. In British and Australian English, you'll find people give a polite preferential nod to towards over toward. However, in the U.S. and Canada, we independently and unabashedly use *toward* more often than *towards*. Technically, either is correct in any situation, however, my rule is: use whichever word sounds right in each situation; it's up to you.

The AP Stylebook is no toward coward; AP states toward is always correct and towards is always a syntactical faux pas. While I appreciate the AP's all-or-nothing approach, I don't think it's necessary to take a stand on every issue. Forgive me for my untowardness.

Is it weird that *coward* and *towered* rhyme? I think these words are messing with me. These two words could lead me to ward off either of these words from my writing for a year (at least).

In the same way American English prefers *toward,* the same rule works with other words related to direction, like *forward, backward, downward, upward* and *afterward.* Again, technically both are acceptable, but *downward* is preferable to *downwards.*

To remember this rule, think about how Americans like our words as we like our drive-thrus: shorter, faster, more convenient and more efficient. Taking an axe to the *s* to make a word one letter shorter is the American way. Does that make us seem backward, or are we moving toward an enlightened state of simplicity and brevity? Either way, it saves one letter on our Twitter character counts, so I'll take it.

○ ○ ○ ○ ○

After all, we're the best.

Americans like being the best at things. We're the best at baseball, jazz, freedom, national parks—pretty much anything Ken Burns has already covered. Yes, living in the Land of Oprah-tunity is glorious. Now, I'd like to award us (and, by us, I mean U.S.) a super-sized gold medal for smashing words together more efficiently than anyone else in the world.

Because Americans value efficiency, we combine multiple words into one super word. One way we do this is through contractions. Don't worry—I'm not talking about the kind of contractions that lead to babies. I'm talking about combining two words to make one short word. These words include don't (do not), we've (we have), and can't (can not). Yes, contractions increase our efficiency so we have more time to manage our burgeoning stock portfolios while refilling our Big Gulps (for free). But some contractions can be tricky.

Have you ever been tripped up by *should've?* *Should've* is a contraction for *should have*. For example:

I should've worn sunscreen when we were at the zoo.

This is a truism for me even on cloudy days. I can get a sunburn through a t-shirt during a solar eclipse.

What about *should of?* As Americans, sometimes we talk so quickly, we say things like *shoulda,* which is an even shorter way of saying *should've*. Many people mistakenly think this phrase is *should of. Should of* is incorrect and should never be spoken, typed, or otherwise communicated. The same rule applies for *must've* (not *must of*), *could've* (not *could of*), and *would've* (not *would of*).

If people you care about use *should of,* wait until you have some one-on-one time with them, calmly sit them down, and then gently correct them. Please don't correct them in public; that's the quickest way to lose friends and end up with a house full of cats (I believe the politically correct term is "fur babies").

In general, contractions like *should've* are still regarded as informal speech, so, if you're writing your doctoral dissertation or cover letter to be hired as a lawyer, avoid these shortcut words. However, in everyday conversations, feel free to contract away. After all, the first amendment grants us free speech, and, since it's the first one, that probably means that it's the best.

○ ○ ○ ○ ○

Blame Noah Webster

Why are so many British and American English words spelled[2] differently? Look no further than the All-American boy Noah Webster, Jr. In addition to being buddies with Alexander Hamilton, serving in the Connecticut House of Representatives, and being a fascinating character, Webster was a lexicographer, which is a fancy way of saying "word nerd." In 1806 he published his first dictionary, called *A Compendious Dictionary of the English Language.*

Much of Webster's influence came from his spelling reform. While spelling reform doesn't sound all that revolutionary, I appreciate Webster's American view of questioning the way things had always been done. Although he introduced many ideas of different and simplified ways to spell words, Webster gets credit for *defense* (instead of *defence*), *color* (instead of *colour*), and *plow* (instead of *plough*). His 1828 *An American Dictionary of the English Language* was Webster's first comprehensive dictionary. It established many of the spelling differences between British and American English, although many other simplifications (like *tung* instead of *tongue* and *soop* instead of *soup*) didn't catch on.

Webster died while working on the second edition of his comprehensive dictionary, at which point the Merriam brothers bought the rights to the project. Thus, the Merriam-Webster Dictionary was born. I can't wait for the Lin-Manuel Miranda musical version of this thrilling American story.

---

2   ...or "spelt," if you're a Brit or an Aussie.

Let's talk about tea

It may be my British roots, but I've never preferred coffee. I like hanging out in coffee shops. I don't mind smelling like I've hung out in a coffee shop all day. But, for me, I like tea. Every morning I need my Barry's Irish Breakfast Tea with a dash of milk and sugar. Without this, I will be a Grumpy Gus or a full-on Fussy Francis. Don't give me Lipton or Twining's—these are not the same. In case you were wondering: yes, I do bring Barry's Irish Breakfast Tea with me when I go out of town.[3] While I like a good morning cuppa, I've never understood kombucha tea.

What is kombucha, anyway? I know you were already thinking about it. *Kombucha* sounds like either someone sneezing or the thing someone says after someone sneezes. Kombucha is like the kale of liquids. Does anyone really enjoy it? If you take a swig of this fermented swill you'll get a mouthful of vinegary, yeasty tea fungus. Sign me up.

I guess I don't like my teas fermented in the same way I don't like my sentences fragmented. Or do I?

The grammar gods strongly advise against writing sentences in fragments. "Sentence fragments" is industry-speak for "incomplete sentences." A complete sentence includes a verb, makes sense on its own, and communicates a complete idea. After all, writing is all about communication.

Here's an example of a sentence fragment:

Because he lives near the ocean.

If the sentence read, "He lives near the ocean," we'd be in good shape. However, adding "Because" to the beginning makes this fragment a dependent clause. We need the "why" to follow the "because." Let's finish that sentence:

---

3 In general, though, I try to avoid leaving home.

Because he lives near the ocean, he collects shells that look like Abraham Lincoln.

That's completely strange; it's also a complete sentence.

Using complete sentences shows that you have a grasp on proper writing rules. Poet Robert Graves said, "Every English poet should master the rules of grammar before he attempts to bend or break them." I agree with this sentiment. Once we comprehend the "proper" way to write, we can break the rules if it helps us better or more accurately express our ideas.

We speak in fragments. Constantly. We use them either to express a casual style, to create rhythm in our writing or to emphasize a point. I agree with Bobby Graves, though: you've got to know the rules before you break them. Seriously.

While grammar purists will probably beg to differ, I will throw them this bone: avoid using sentence fragments in formal writing. If you're writing your doctoral dissertation, stay away from sentence fragments. However, when you are writing in a conversational, informal forum, feel free to play with the rules.

Just as some people like their tea slightly fermented, some people like their sentences lightly fragmented. It adds an interesting flavor to an otherwise conventional cup of language libation. While I don't prefer kombucha, I don't have a problem with those who fancy effervescent fungus tea.

What in the word?

Born is when something or someone is birthed.
Borne is the past participle of the verb *bear* (not the animal).
Bourne is a CIA operative who got brainwashed and became a secret super agent.

Jumping over life's rattlesnakes and mountain lions.

That's the way I live my life; I grip it and rip it.
—Hansel, Zoolander

I think we have a strong, American impulse that tells us to do something despite someone else's warning not to do that exact thing. I'm sure someone cautioned motorcycle stuntman Evel Knievel against attempting a dangerous motorcycle jump over a box of 50 rattlesnakes followed by 2 mountain lions in 1965, but he did it anyway. I suppose it doesn't matter that he bumped into the edge of the box of snakes when he landed, causing the onlookers to scramble for their lives, because this stunt literally launched Knievel's career as an entertainer and household name.

Now it's time to launch into our next grammar lesson. When should you use *anyway* and when should you use *any way*? And is *anyways* ever acceptable? Let's jump in.

Anyway means "in any case" or "regardless."

> Even though many people warned him, Evel Knievel attempted to jump across the canyon anyway.

You can also use *anyway* to signal you're continuing a story that was interrupted.

> "So, anyway, I told the guy, 'That's not even my dog!'" Jeff joked.

When it comes to *any way* as two words, the rules are different. The word *any* modifies *way*. *Any way* means "by any manner" or "by any method." For example:

> There wasn't any way the rattlesnakes were going to go back into the box voluntarily.

> In order to get my kids to go to sleep at night, I'll bribe

them in any way I can.

Anyways is a nonstandard, or colloquial, way of saying *anyway*. I wouldn't advise you to use it in a formal speech (while delivering a eulogy or a State of the Union address), but it's not necessarily wrong. Use it only in informal speech or writing.

However, as soon as I try to forbid you from using *anyways* in your lexicon, you're totally going to do it. It was the same when someone told Evel Kneivel he couldn't jump over 50 cars—he did it anyway. As soon as anyone attempts to limit the American psyche or tell us we can't do something, we answer the doubters and haters by saying, "Just watch me." Just make sure the snakes stay in their box this time.

○ ○ ○ ○ ○

All that glitters is gold; only superstars break the mold.

I had a friend visit me the other day to tell me about a problem. I listened to her secret shame and consoled her. Under the veil of anonymity, she agreed to allow me to use her issue, but not her real name. For our purposes, we'll call her Gwenifer.

Gwenifer didn't know whether to use the word *medal* or *metal* in an email she was typing. When I reminded her of the existence of *meddle* and *mettle*, her brain nearly exploded. I'm afraid that's not what she needed in her moment of uncertainty.

Medal, metal, meddle and *mettle* are examples of homophones, types of homonyms that sound alike, have different meanings, and also have different spellings. It's no wonder Gwenifer became confused; *medal* and *metal* have some crossover meanings.

Metal is a substance like gold, silver or copper that is usually hard and shiny. Metals are malleable and have excellent thermal and electrical conductivity properties. Other examples of metals include aluminum, iron, and bronze. We get the word *metal* from the Latin word *metallum*, meaning quarry, mine, or metal.

Confusingly, a medal is always made of metal. In the Olympics, the top three contestants win gold, silver and bronze medals, respectively. A medal is a flattened piece of metal, often in the shape of a circle, to commemorate or honor someone. The word *medal* originates from the Latin word *medallia*, which was a coin worth half a denarius.

Meddle is when you get all up in someone else's business, to borrow from a common colloquialism. *Meddle* means getting involved in another person's matters without (and often against) her consent.

> Gwenifer's nosy neighbor Nina often meddles when she gives Gwenifer unwelcome relationship advice.

We get our modern English word *meddle* from an Old English word *medler*, which meant "to mix."

What does *mettle* mean, and how did we get it? It simply means courage or fortitude. Mettle speaks of a brave person's unwavering temperament. If it sounds similar to *metal*, that's because *mettle* originated from a metaphorical version of metal. In the mid-sixteenth century, the word *mettle* shows up as a specialized spelling of the word *metal*, and should only be used for figurative uses.

I don't fault folks like Gwenifer when they trip over these incredibly similar words; that's why I didn't even mention *pedal, petal, peddle* and *pettle*. Those are homophones for another lesson.

○ ○ ○ ○ ○

Don't be basic

What's a phrasal verb, and how can it make my life better? Those are fair questions, especially because it's possible you've never heard of a phrasal verb.

I have a hunch you can figure out what it is. Think about *phrasal*. This will probably have something to do with a saying that involves multiple words. Phrases are frequently used in colloquial (or casual) language and conversation. How about *verb*? This probably means a phrasal verb will contain (you guessed it) a verb. To quote Karen from *Mean Girls*: "I'm a mouse, duh!"

If *Mean Girls* has taught us anything, it's that we shouldn't try to be "basic," which is a pejorative term for a girl who flits from one trend to the next based on whatever the Instagram influencer of the moment is getting paid to promote. The most basic thing is to order a PSL (pumpkin spice latte) from Starbucks the first day it's available (usually during late summer). For the record, as I write this, I *am* drinking a pumpkin spice chai latte during late summer, but I'm at a local coffee shop (Noble Coffee and Tea in downtown Noblesville, Indiana, for those of you who were wondering. Support local businesses!). You do you; don't let someone else dictate who you should be, unless that's what you want to do, or unless it's a role model like Jesus, Oprah, Mr. Rogers or Katniss Everdeen. The point is, it's up to you.

Now, let's get back to phrasal verbs: a phrasal verb is a phrase that uses two or three words consisting of a verb and a particle and/or a preposition to form one semantic unit. Phrasal verbs are also known as *verbal idioms*, if that helps you understand the term better.

The easiest way to understand phrasal verbs is to share some examples: turn up, back off, tune out, hook up, play along and lean in. Now that you see this list, you probably realize we use phrasal verbs all the time.

What I find fascinating about phrasal verbs is that you can

start with one base verb (let's use *blow*) and, by adding different prepositions, you end up with completely different meanings: blow up, blow in, blow off, blow out. All those phrases have unique meanings. You take one basic verb and "jazz it up" with a punchy preposition. Verbs on their own are so basic.

On the other hand, some phrasal verbs with the same base verbs mean almost the same thing: back off, back away, back down. Those phrasal verbs all have something to do with retreating.

As we've already established, phrasal verbs are informal, which means you have to memorize what they mean. Non-native English speakers may have a hard time with these, as they are a form of idiom. Recognizing and understanding idioms necessitates a contextual knowledge of culture and surroundings. All that to say, you have to "bone up on" your phrasal verbs.

My favorite thing about phrasal verbs? You can end a sentence with one, which means (at least in this case) it's kosher to end a sentence with a preposition. So, lighten up. Calm down. Chill out. Phrasal verbs are part of our everyday language, and they're not falling out of fashion anytime soon. Thanks for letting me geek out.

○ ○ ○ ○ ○

Things you hope never to use in life

I can think of a few things off the top of my head that I hope never to use: math, a fire extinguisher, Pepto Bismol, and the flotation device on the bottom of my seat cushion on an airplane. In theory, all of these things are good to have or know about, but you hope you're never in a situation where they're necessary for your survival.

In the same way, it seems like people avoid using quotation marks correctly. And, rightfully so: these punctuation marks look like a pair of commas who have pumped themselves full of helium. But I try to look at it this way: quotation marks are up there to give your words a high five.

Let's start with the basics. Use quotation marks around dialogue (i.e., something someone says).

> "I'm still upset Pluto is no longer a planet," Humphrey remarked.

This is an example of a direct quote, so it gets quotation marks. However, consider the following sentence:

> Humphrey remarked he was still upset Pluto is no longer a planet.

This is an example of an indirect quote, so it doesn't require quotation marks.

I like to think of quotation marks as T. rex fingers, demarcating the words inside as special, kind of like the lucky underwear you only wear when you want to have an exceptionally awesome day.

So, what else gets the quotation mark treatment? In addition to dialogue, A.P. style instructs us to put quotation marks around the titles of books, songs, television shows, computer games, poems, lectures, speeches and works of art. Do not, however, put quotation marks around the names of magazines, newspapers, the Bible or books that are catalogs of reference materials. As I mentioned earlier, I don't see eye-to-eye with the A.P. folks' distinction between quotation marks and italics.

Finally, use quotation marks to indicate something is unusual, novel, ironic, or sarcastic. For instance:

> NASA continues to make us believe in the so-called "moon landing."

For the record, I didn't say this, but I have a friend (let's call him "Byron") who thinks the moon landing is a hoax. Byron uses ironic and sarcastic quotation marks all the time when referring to the various conspiracy theories to which he subscribes.

Here's the bottom line: you should learn how to use quotation marks correctly. They may not save your life, but well-placed quotation marks make the words inside them feel like they're at a super deluxe, exclusive syntax party. Fancy!

What in the word?

A *click* is a sharp sound.
A *clique* is an exclusive group of people, usually comprised of mean girls. Often the leader is named Megan (pronounced MEE-gan, and she *will* correct you if you say it wrong).

Irregular animals

It's time to take a look at the strange plural nounimal kingdom. Now, I know "nounimal" isn't a word (yet), but I'm convinced one of my made-up words will catch on eventually.

I was going to write an entire essay on irregular plural nouns, that is, nouns that don't follow traditional rules of pluralization. The more I got into it, the more I found that animals break the rules way more than other nouns. Why is that? Maybe it's because they're animals, and most of them haven't yet learned to speak English.

With most nouns, you can simply add an *-s* or *-es* to the end of them to make them plural. Not so with irregular nouns. There's an entire category of irregular plural nouns whose singular form end in *f*, but to make them plural you take away the *f* and add *-ves*. In the animal category, *calf* and *wolf* become *calves* and *wolves*.

A second category of irregular nouns is made plural by changing vowels, changing the word, or adding a different ending altogether. These (in the animal kingdom) include *mouse/mice, ox/oxen,* and *goose/geese.*

But if *goose* becomes *geese,* why doesn't *moose* become *meese?* These nouns are wild; they don't follow the rules. That leads us to a big category of nouns that simply stay the same when pluralized. The list includes most fish like salmon, shrimp, cod, tuna and trout, other animals like bison, elk, deer, sheep, swine, buffalo, quail and antelope. Some of these also have traditional -*s* and -*es* endings viewed as acceptable by whichever governing body makes and breaks the plural rules of English (do they go by a majority vote or simply a plurality?). It's total nounsense.

Normally I'd offer some kind of rule to help you remember each animal's plural forms. What's the best way to remember these? Practice. Imagine poor Noah, loading up the ark with all these animals' persnickety plural forms. At a certain point he probably simply grouped them all by species, when he thought to himself: what's the plural of species? Species. Oh, deer.

○ ○ ○ ○ ○

Go heavy on the sunscreen...

Did you know that redheaded people make up only 1–2% of the world's population? There's a reason we are so scarce: the sun. I'm that person who can get a sunburn on a cloudy day. People have been known to get secondhand sunburns by just standing near me outside on a sunny day. I'm so white I get a moonburn. I'm like a vampire or something—I step out into the light of day and basically just burst into flames. This is why I always apply sunscreen; I apply it early and often.

If you noticed, I used a few adverbs just now (always, early, often). Not only did I employ a handful of adverbs, but I used a handful of adverbs of frequency. Adverbs of frequency describe how often something happens. They include always, normally, usually, sometimes, never, frequently, often, then and weekly. And, I have more good news for you: adverbs of frequency come with their own set of rules.

When your sentence has more than one verb, use your adverb of frequency before the primary verb. Here's an example:

> I have often received a sunburn during the month of November.

Here, we sandwiched our adverb of frequency (often) between the bread slices of our sentence's two verbs (have and received).

If your sentence contains only one verb, place your adverb of frequency after your subject and before your verb.

> Curtis never tans. He always wears a swim shirt to the pool.

We use adverbs of frequency to signify things that happen on a routine basis. Because of this, we usually employ these adverbs with the present simple tense.

If you want to "throw shade," as the youths say, when you're using an adverb of frequency in a negative context while forming a question, place your adverb before your primary verb:

> Are you normally so angry, or are you just like this on days that end in -*ay*?

Most of the time, place definite adverbs of frequency (including finally, last week, today, monthly, and already) either at the beginning or at the end of your sentence. When the adverb is the focus of your sentence, save it for the end:

I will do the laundry tomorrow.

When it's not the emphasis of your sentence, use a definite adverb of frequency at the beginning:

Sometimes I wonder if I'll ever do laundry again.

Practicing good grammar—much like applying sunscreen—is a fantastic life decision. I encourage you to do it early and often.

Here's a guide to adverbs of frequency show with the approximate percentage of time they convey.

Frequency	Adverb of Frequency	Example
100%	always	I always drink tea in the morning.
90%	usually	I usually remember to shower.
80%	normally/ generally	I normally brush my teeth.
70%	often/ frequently	I frequently lose my keys.
50%	sometimes	I sometimes smell the milk before I pour it.
30%	occasionally	I occasionally forget to put on new socks.
10%	seldom	I seldom leave the house without my travel mug.
5%	hardly ever/ rarely	I rarely want to leave the house.

| 0% | never | I never leave the house without my Burt's Bees lip balm. |

○ ○ ○ ○ ○

...but go easy on the mustard

I like mustard so much that I'm considering getting a mustard fridge.

Have you ever put spicy mustard on a sandwich? If you inadvertently glob on too much of the good stuff, you'll swear you just snorted wasabi. When it comes to spices that are in your face (literally and figuratively), a little bit can go a long way.

In the same way, hyphens and dashes—when sprinkled into sentences properly—add just the right punch. Not only are we about to learn how to use the hyphen (-) properly, but we're also going to learn how to use both the en (–) and em (—) dashes.

Let's start with hyphens. Hyphens are like glue for two words that are connected. Use hyphens in compound adjectives, which are adjectives that precede a noun they modify in order to connect them together. Examples of compound adjectives include *well-known, blue-haired, one-eyed,* and *ill-conceived.* Hyphens are also used to separate numbers (three hundred sixty-five) and to create a line break when syllables of the same word get separated. We still see this sometimes in books and newspapers, but we see it less often now that text is not set by hand.

En dashes (–) are all about range. Use an en dash in order to show a range of numbers.

Barack Obama was president from 2008–2016.

The Thunder beat the Jazz 120–101.

The store is open Monday–Friday, 9:00 a.m.–5:00 p.m.

The en dash is named as such because it is about the width of the letter *n*. To type an en dash on a PC, press CTRL+minus. For PC laptops without numeric keyboards, you can type ALT+0150 or insert-special characters in Word. On a Mac, press option+hyphen.

The em dash (—) is the length of the letter *m*. Generally use it as a more dramatic substitute for other punctuation, like commas, colons, semicolons or parentheses.

Do not—I repeat—do not put spaces around the em dash; allow the words to bump up right next to the em dash to show the immediacy and drama it interjects.

To type an em dash on a PC, press ALT+CTRL+minus. For PC laptops without numeric keyboards, you can type ALT+0151 or insert-special characters in Word. On a Mac, press option+shift+hyphen.

Dashes and hyphens are generally used incorrectly because, in order to use them correctly, you have to know the right way to employ them. If you want to get a shiny gold star sticker on your grammar chart, learn the difference between hyphens, en dashes and em dashes.

Mustard is a must.

"The road to hell is paved with adverbs."
—Stephen King

What's a sandwich without a little sauce? And, by sauce, of course, I mean mustard. Without mustard, a sandwich is dry, boring and lifeless. Please, I don't want any emails from the pro-mayo lobby on this one. For me, it's mustard or bust.

Adverbs are like sentence mustard. They add flavor and intensity to otherwise plain word sandwiches. An adverb is a word that modifies a verb, adjective, another adverb, or an entire sentence or clause. Most of us think of adverbs being words that always end in -*ly*. The fact is, many adverbs do end in -*ly*.

Sam walked slowly to school.

Hampton chortled heartily at Peggy's pun.

I frequently check my email.

On the other hand, there's a long list of adverbs that do not end in -*ly*. Keep these words in mind the next time you play Mad Libs on a road trip: they include afterward, never, next, often, and almost. These adverbs are like the honey mustard of sandwich condiments; you might not even think you're eating mustard because they're so sweet and discreet.

Adverbs never modify nouns—that's a job strictly reserved for adjectives. Adjectives are like sentence cheese to the noun's meat; they make sure the adverb doesn't touch the noun. You do put the mustard on top of the cheese and not directly on the meat, right? We're not barbarians, after all.

The further I go into this metaphor, the hungrier I get. In this case, I suppose verbs are veggie toppings like lettuce, tomato, and probably pickles (although I'm personally not a pickle person).

Adverbs give additional information about when, where or how something happens. How did Kenny run? Kenny ran quickly. When did Byron start doubting the moon landing? Byron started doubting the moon landing yesterday. How frequently do you read the newspaper? I read the newspaper often.

Once you start noticing adverbs, you'll see them everywhere. It's similar to buying a car—prior to buying the car, you don't notice many of the same models on the road, but after you buy it, you see your same car everywhere. Just be careful not to spill any mustard on your new interior.

What in the word?

Bated is something that is diminished: I waited with bated breath. *Baited* is what happens after you put a worm on a hook or when you bother someone incessantly. I suppose the only thing that can have *baited* breath is a fish once the wormy hook is in its mouth.

How to achieve a higher level of consciousness

Are you wound up? Worked up? Burnt out? Are you tired of being tired? Do you have outrage fatigue from whatever political scandal is dominating today's headlines? Believe it or not, we weren't born with smartphones and social media connected to our wrists 24/7. We are growing increasingly anxious as a culture. It's time to disconnect from our unsustainable, frenzied existences for a minute to calm our overwrought brains.

Can I make a suggestion? Try a simple breathing exercise for five minutes. Get alone, close your eyes and take some deep breaths. Put your phone away. Pay attention to your breath and watch your anxiety meter drop down a few notches.

Only when we make an intentional effort to slow down can we achieve higher levels of consciousness—or is it conscience? Unconscious? Let's clear up the differences between these confusing words.

Conscience is a noun that refers to someone's internal sense of right and wrong. When you steal paperclips from the office to make chainmail for your fashion-forward upcycled clothing line, your conscience is the thing that makes you feel a little guilty for pilfering $27 worth of office products. The adjective version of *conscience* is *conscientious*, which means that someone is guided by her sense of right and wrong, careful not to make mistakes.

Conscious is an adjective that means to be aware, alert, intentional or awake. Before your alarm goes off in the morning, you're unconscious (most people call this "sleeping"). If you make a conscious effort to make eye contact and be present with people, that means you're taking intentional steps to change your behavior for the better. If someone is self-conscious, that means he is aware of how he perceives others view him.

Being self-conscious can mean being self-aware; in negative connotations, however, being self-conscious can make someone hyper-aware of how others view himself to the point of paranoia. Be self-conscious in a good way.

The term *consciousness* is a noun that has to do with the state of being conscious. It is a deep level of thoughtfulness that helps people become more aware of themselves and others.

I'll offer one cautionary note before you begin your intentional breathing exercises: if your surroundings are too dark, you're likely to slip into unconsciousness before you can gain a sense of higher consciousness. On the other hand, you look like you could use a nap, so make sure to set the alarm on your smartphone.

What in the word?

To *home in* on a target means to move directly toward something.
Hone means to sharpen or make more accurate.
Although many people use *hone in*, that phrase is not correct.
The correct phrase is *home in*.
Introverts often refer to an ideal Friday night as a *home-in*.

Stay in school

During the spring semester of my junior year in college at the University of Oklahoma (Boomer Sooner!), I came down with a mystery virus. Its symptoms were similar to mono, but it wasn't mono. I was tired all the time, had a headache and other general swelling and other unpleasantries. I could barely get out of bed. My doctor concluded that I had a virus. Which virus was it? That was a tough one.

I got tested for every virus known to mankind. The mean people took my blood in vial after vial, only to come back with negative tests. In the meantime, I was missing classes. After a few weeks of this, I had to file for an "incomplete" in each of my 15 credit hours of classes, to be made up over the next year with each professor on an individual basis.

I'll never forget what my doctor told me while we were trying to figure out what I had. He said, "Good news; either your body will fight off and kill this virus, or it'll kill you." Wait, what? I'm pretty sure this is how the actual zombie apocalypse will start.

The entire medical community was stumped as to what was happening inside my body.

While I stayed quarantined in my one-bedroom apartment for most of that semester, my doctor gave me some pretty strong meds. I had a friend who, at the time, was a cable guy (back when cable was still a thing). He connected a wire that gave me all the channels, and I stumbled upon daily marathons of *In Living Color* on BET. I'd watch four hours in a row while lying in a semi-conscious state of entertained stupor.

One night I looked out my back window to find a possum hanging out on my back balcony, upon which I had recently installed an "outdoor couch."[4] My trespassing possum wouldn't go away, and I had no weapons to force it off my balcony. Heavily

---

4   This is just as classy as it sounds. After the first time it rained, the couch was basically a foamy cesspool of mold and fungi.

medicated, I decided the best way to get rid of an unwanted balcony possum was to throw ice cubes at it. I'd quickly open the door just enough to pelt the nocturnal nuisance, but not wide enough to let it spring in and bite me, infecting me with possum rabies. I'm pretty sure this is how the actual zombie apocalypse will start.

Slowly, my symptoms dissipated. I was able to reenter society and resume rubbing shoulders with fellow humans. My body did kill the virus, although it was a long war of attrition. I almost didn't graduate, but I put in a ton of work during my senior year to complete all my required coursework. This brings me to a weird word usage situation I've heard quite a bit: do people *graduate college* or *graduate from college*?

You would never say "I sat floor" or "He arrived Oklahoma," would you? That sounds ridiculous. "I graduated" on its own is a complete sentence. So is "I sat" or "He arrived." These are short, but sweet, complete sentences.

The key here is that "graduated" in the sentence "I graduated from college," operates as an intransitive verb, which doesn't allow or take a direct object. Here's an example of a transitive verb sentence: Byron launched the cat into orbit. Here, "launched" is a transitive verb. Not only is it an active verb, but it also allows for at least one direct object (in this instance only one). The direct object here (cat) receives the action (launched) from the subject (Byron).

So, now let's look at why "I graduated college" doesn't work. For the sentence to pass muster, "college" would need to be a direct object. That would mean the direct object (college) receives the action (graduated) from the subject (I). This just doesn't make sense.

Now let's look at why "I graduated from college" does work. Here, "graduated" functions as an intransitive verb; it doesn't take a direct object. Fellow word nerds already recognize "from college" as a prepositional phrase in which "from" is the preposition and "college" is the prepositional object. Now this sentence works!

If you or a loved one hold a graduation open house, make sure you don't say "I graduated college." The dean of your school might hear you and decide to shred your diploma. This sounds unlikely, but so does the zombie apocalypse, and I almost started it. Twice.

○ ○ ○ ○ ○

How to conquer the farmers market

I love early summer for many reasons, but perhaps my favorite thing about this particular season is the farmers market. I make sure to stock up on kettle corn, sweet corn, cornhole bags, candy corn, and top off my peppercorn grinder. What can I say? In Indiana, we love our corn.

But the question of the moment is: does *farmers market* need an apostrophe in it? We have three contending spellings vying for the top spot: farmers market, farmer's market, and farmers' market. Which is it?

Farmers market is what the AP Stylebook considers a descriptive phrase (as opposed to a possessive phrase). In general, the farmers do not own the market, nor does one sole farmer. And, as far as I know, they're not selling farmers at the market. It's a market for farmers, not a market that belongs to farmers.

Use an apostrophe when *of* would be an accurate longer form possessive phrase. For example: Newton's law. This is a law of Newton. Victoria's Secret is a secret of, or belonging to, Victoria.

For descriptive phrases, you don't need an apostrophe when *for* or *by* are accurate longer form phrases. For example: Colts quarterback is a quarterback for the Colts. A teachers college is a college for teachers. In these cases, the plural noun (farmers, Colts, or teachers) function as adjectives to describe what kind of market, quarterback, or school you're discussing.

Now for some exceptions (because English is fun)! Descriptive phrases such as women's rugby get an apostrophe because the plural *women* doesn't end in the letter *s*. Other examples include children's hospital (the children certainly don't own the hospital) and men's restroom.

Of course, the Chicago Manual of Style people disagree with the AP Style crew. It's a classic "Sharks vs. Jets" back alley knife fight scenario where the two rival factions never seem to see eye-to-eye; instead, they'll just do fierce, synchronized snapping around each other to attempt to intimidate the other gang. I couldn't find a great explanation as to why the Chicago Manual of Style prefers *farmers' market*, but they just do.

As long as my local farmers market is always well-stocked with corn-related items, I don't think I'll complain if I see a rogue apostrophe on its sign; besides, apostrophes are just commas giving high fives. I do, however, personally think the term *farmers market* as a descriptive phrase does not require an apostrophe.

○ ○ ○ ○ ○

Candy corn is not a vegetable

Yes, I am a proud naturalized Hoosier. Although I was born and raised in Oklahoma, I've lived in Indiana for over a decade. If I've learned one thing during my time here, it's this: Indiana loves corn. As a Midwesterner, I have an intense fondness for corn dogs, cornucopias, popcorn, cornbread, unicorns, cornerbacks, and even candy corn. And, although it pains me to say this, candy corn is not a vegetable. Don't fool yourself, people.

What about eggcorns?

I'm not talking about some kind of newfangled, lab-based, hypoallergenic superfood; an eggcorn is an unintentional word substitution we sometimes make in a phrase because we misunderstand or mishear the original phrase. The eggcorn got its name from linguistics professor Geoffrey Pullum in 2003, when he came across an article on Mark Liberman's linguistics blog, *Language Log*, that discussed a woman who substituted the phrase *egg corn* for the word *acorn*. Pullum suggested that the linguistics community start referring to these phrases as *eggcorns*. The moniker stuck.

The difference between an eggcorn and a pun is that a pun is intentional; to the eggcorn utterer, the phrase may be an unintentionally clever way of relaying a misunderstood phrase. Here are some examples: *pass mustard* instead of *pass muster, escape goat* instead of *scapegoat, bond fire* instead of *bonfire, flush out* instead of *flesh out*, and *mute point* instead of *moot point*.

As you can see, these phrases actually make sense, although they're technically incorrect. I had a coworker (let's call her Nadine) who unknowingly deployed eggcorns all the time. Since I didn't know what an eggcorn was, I used to refer to these phrases as "Nadinisms." She would probably accuse me of being a "rebel rouser" for putting this in print. Just know I've changed her name here because, as Nadine used to say, "it takes two to tangle." She really had a "sick sense" for eggcorns.

I hope I've "wet your appetite" to think of some more eggcorns. There certainly are a "wild variety" of them. Please note I've put all eggcorns in this article in "flotation marks" so that you know you're not seeing an "optical delusion." I just wanted to "nip that in the butt" so you didn't "take it for granite" that the Grammar Guy would ever make such an egregious error; that would certainly be "disconcerning."

What in the word?

A *leek* is an onion's hoity-toity foreign exchange student vegetable cousin.
A *leak* is when you've got a hole in your bucket.
Leke is a town in Belgium.

Just try not to die.

Falling coconuts kill an estimated 150 people worldwide every year. Because I don't want to get killed by a falling coconut, I'm working on a patent for a combination shield/umbrella, which I'm thinking about calling the shumbrella (coming soon to a Bed Bath and Beyond near you). Falling from a height of 80 feet, coconuts can reach speeds of 50 miles per hour. And, even though I haven't noticed any coconut trees in Indiana (yet), a coconut could fall out of a plane, get shot out of a cannon or spat out of a really intense geyser, make an impact with my head and kill me. It could happen.

What I really want to know is, when talking about my chances of getting killed by a falling coconut, should I use *may* or *might*? Is it "I may die as a result of the impact of a falling coconut" or "I might die as a result of the impact of a falling coconut?"

When it comes to *may* vs. *might*, it's a matter of likelihood. If something *may* happen, it's more likely than something that *might* happen. The incredibly unscientific way I remember which one to use is: may = yay; might = yeah right. As in, *may* could likely happen (yay) and *might* has a much smaller probability of occurring (yeah right).

Based on an incredibly small likelihood, I would correctly say I *might* die as a result of the impact of a falling coconut. As a left-handed person, I'm much more likely to die from operating a product intended for right-handed people. It happens to approximately 2,500 southpaws each year. And, with my poor track record using traditional, right-handed can openers, I would correctly say I *may* die while improperly operating equipment intended for right-handed users.

I'm actually a little worried about the statistic about equipment killing lefties. After all, at 10% of the world's population, our quantities are already limited. Let's just say I'm unlikely to operate a chainsaw anytime soon; I might use a chainsaw, but I probably won't.

Interlude: Have the best words.

No matter what anybody tells you, words and ideas can change the world.
—Robin Williams as John Keating, Dead Poets Society

I have a five-year-old son. Right now toilet humor is big. Body parts are funny. Things that produce bad smells get big laughs. Basically, I'm in my comedic sweet spot when I'm with the pre-K crowd. Apparently, I act my shoe size more often than I act my age. I'm okay with that.

Guess what, fellow word nerds? According to a 2017 Springer Study that surveyed 821 participants, English speakers, as a whole, aren't any more mature than I am. The study asked participants to rate 211 words on a scale of 1 to 5, where 1 is not funny at all and 5 is downright hilarious. In total, the participants ranked nearly 5,000 words.

Let me cut to the chase and give you the top 10 funniest words in the English language in order of hilarity: booty, tit, booby, hooter, nitwit, twit, waddle, tinkle, bebop, and egghead. I can safely guarantee this collection of words will never appear together in the same sentence again, although, if they did, they'd get tons of guffaws and chortles, based on the data.

Before you dismiss this list of funniest words, just know that 58% of respondents were women. The average age of participants was 35. 70% of people who participated in the study had at least completed an undergraduate degree. So that means we can definitively say *booty* is a word people can't help but find funny. My five-year-old and I would certainly agree.

Whether you're an egghead or a nitwit, isn't it comforting to know we giggle at the same things? Republicans and Democrats both snicker when someone says *tinkle*. Black and white people alike agree that *waddle* is chuckleworthy. Our collective immaturity gives me hope that we are more alike than we are different. That gives me hope.

Comedic words won't necessarily fix our disagreements, but I do think they can help. So, the next time you find yourself in a frustrating ideological argument with a Twitter troll or your crazy drunk uncle, I recommend casually dropping in a few of these words into your conversation. Just don't accuse the other person of resembling one of these words; if you do, you might end up on the receiving end of a swift kick to the keister...or booty.

○ ○ ○ ○ ○

Here are the worst words

No one likes the word *moist*. I also find the following words to be particularly icky: *cyst, pus, dipthong, dongle, ointment, seepage, yeasty, analgesic, succulent, kumquat,* and *goiter.* There's even a relatively-new word for the disgust of certain words: *logomisia.* This word is so new that it's not in most dictionaries. Perhaps the pencil-pushers over at the big dictionary companies have logomisia for the word *logomisia.*

Speaking of hating certain words, I'm afraid you're not going to like this.

I love to ask people what their least favorite word is (for the record, mine is *supple*). By far, according to my informal surveying tactics, the word that gets the most votes is *irregardless*.

I'm sorry to break it to you, but *irregardless* is *technically* a word.

Yes, *irregardless* is a word. Depending on the word processing tool you use, it sometimes gets the red squiggly underline treatment—but not always. And if you look up *irregardless* in a dictionary, you'll find it there along with all of the other officially-sanctioned words.

When people jokingly use *irregardless*, they are doing it wrong. Those who utter it accompanied by an ironic smirk simply use it instead of *regardless*, to the frustration of word purists.

Many have dismissed the word *irregardless* because they view it as redundant; *regardless* is all we need, they argue. Adding *ir-* in front of *regardless* downright irritates people.

But that's the wrong way to use *irregardless*. You see, *irregardless* is a way to drop the mic on an argument after someone has already used *regardless*. Here's an example:

> **Robin:** Batman, will you let me pick the music on the Bat Radio next time we're in the Batmobile? I promise not to sing along.

> **Batman:** Absolutely not. Regardless, your taste in music is terrible.

> **Robin:** Holy supple salamanders, Batman! I won't play any Creed or Nickelback. Can I pick the music, please?

> **Batman:** Irregardless, my answer is "no." To the Batcave.

In this scene, Batman shuts down the argument by putting extra emphasis on *regardless* by saying *irregardless*. Batman knows how to use *irregardless* properly. Also, he's the one who wears the pants in the Dynamic Duo (okay, technically they're tights, but Robin only wears green underwear).

Most of the time *irregardless* is used, it's misused, probably in a knowingly tongue-in-cheek manner. And its intent comes through; people either get bothered by their friend's usage of *irregardless* or they think it's funny. Either way, unless you're using *irregardless* like Batman, you're doing it wrong.

Batman once said "It's not who I am underneath, but what I do that defines me." I say: leave the defining up to the dictionary; we can all do a better job of improving our grammar and word usage to make our lives more awesome.

○ ○ ○ ○ ○

The best-sounding words

"I know words; I have the best words."
–President Donald Trump

There's an entire school of thinking for beautiful words. It's called *phonaesthetics*. Think about words that sound nice to your eardrums; these words make your brain release oodles of endorphins. Hearing pleasant-sounding words is the aural equivalent of watching baby river otters perform a synchronized swimming routine.

There's a word to describe these pleasant-sounding words: euphonious. Actually, the word *euphonious* is itself euphonious. How about that? Do you know what many people consider to be the most pleasing word out there? *Cellar door*. Okay, *cellar door* isn't one word, but it's a compound word that isn't smooshed together into one word. Respect the space, people! Both J.R.R. Tolkien and C.S. Lewis (two of my favorite Inklings) noted that *cellar door* is one of the most beautiful phrases in the English language. If I ever start an underground spoken word appreciation club, I think I'll name it "The Cellar Door."

Here is a sampling of words that frequent the top of the

charts when phonoaestheticians put together lists of the most euphonious words. For the purposes of this exercise, just imagine I'm reading this list to you in the voice of Liam Neeson: *iridescent, solitude, luminous, lullaby, serendipity, destiny, idyllic, soliloquy,* and *elysian.* As opposed to *cellar door,* these words have incredibly positive connotations.

It's easy to forget that our mutt of a language can be quite lovely when someone strings together a sequence of perfectly elegant-sounding prose. We've become accustomed to being bombarded by political polarization that presents anyone who doesn't agree with you as an enemy. Harsh words abound (just watch your Twitter stream for five minutes). People born after a certain year can't get along with people born before a certain year. Instead of dividing Sharks from Jets, why don't we combine forces to form jet-sharks, the most terrifying, unstoppable air-and-sea threat you'll ever face?

My vote for the best-sounding phrase in the English language is "Here's your pile of cash," although I'd settle for hearing my kids say, "Daddy, we're going to let you go to the bathroom alone without barging in and having a conversation with you." I doubt I'll ever hear either of those statements uttered in my general direction.

Lucky in Love

How good grammar will make you irresistible to attractive people

> *I had someone correct my grammar once on a blind date, and within the first ten minutes the date was over. You just don't correct somebody's grammar. That's just not okay.*
> —*Reese Witherspoon*

In a survey of 1,700 online daters, Kibin (a professional proof-reading service) found that 47% think poor grammar is a "major turn-off," while 35% said that good grammar is "sexy." Women had stronger opinions about grammar than the men who responded.

A similar survey by Zoosk (an online dating service) found that online daters who mention *spelling* in their profiles get up to 73% more incoming messages; those who mention *grammar* get up to 93% more incoming messages. The same study showed that 72% of respondents are turned off by terrible spelling, while 48% of the 9,000 online daters consider bad grammar to be a "deal breaker."

Finally, Grammarly (a company that provides an online digital writing tool) reviewed 10,000 online profiles on the dating site Match.com. Both men and women view good grammar as a more important attribute than confidence. Additionally, men with at least two spelling errors on their online profiles are 14% less likely to get a response.

What can we learn from this information? First of all, it seems like all the good website URLs are taken; in order to start a website, you have to invent a new word. Secondly, good grammar increases your odds at love. The numbers don't lie.

Do you want to woo a celebrity? You might find their grammar standards are higher. According to John Mayer, "Ladies, if you want to know the way to my heart: good spelling and good grammar, good punctuation, capitalize only where you are supposed to capitalize, it's done."[1] The point is, good grammar is a turn on if wielded wisely. You don't want to come across as a dummy. If you "play dumb" to attract dates, you'll find yourself relegated to dating jerks and morons. You're better than that; put your best grammar foot forward and you're likely to find yourself on third dates with attractive smart people who have savings accounts.

The following grammar tips are designed specifically to help you sharpen your romantic prowess. Don't thank me now; you can thank me by sending me an invitation to your wedding.

○ ○ ○ ○ ○

Lessons from *The Bachelor*

If you watch *The Bachelor* (which I most definitely do not), you probably hear the following phrase ad nauseam during the "confessional" videos: "Topher and I's relationship is really

---

1   That's the second John Mayer reference in this book, for those of you keeping score at home. He should really run for mayor. Those campaign signs would be fantastic.

special. I think he may be the one." Then the next girl comes in and says literally the exact same thing.

When you catch yourself saying something similar, don't beat yourself up. It seems like the natural thing to say in the *Bachelor* example, Topher and *I* share a relationship. In order to make Topher possessive (which he totally is, by the way), you would add *'s: Topher's*. Pretty easy.

Now, to make *I* possessive, you actually get rid of it altogether and replace it with *my. My* is the possessive form of *I*. So, to speak or write this sentence correctly, you would say "Topher's and my relationship is really special." I know that sounds awkward, but it's correct. If you want to avoid this awkward linguistic limbo, you can simply say "Our relationship is really special."

When you are referring to two or more other people who share the same thing, you only need to add *-'s* to the last person listed. So, if you're a contestant on *The Bachelor* and you are referring to another girl's relationship with our boy Topher, you would write/say: "Topher and Krystyn's relationship makes me totally want to hurl. Please pass the champagne." Even though that's a terrible way to spell Kristen, it's a grammatically correct sentence.

In the case of multiple owners who have separate ownership, you add *-'s* to each name. Krystyn and Ashlee each have a different relationship with Topher, so if you were griping about their relationships, you'd say something like: "Krystyn's and Ashlee's relationships with Topher make me totally want to eat my feelings. Please pass the ice cream."

This grammar terminology of compound ownership is called compound, or joint, possession. And, while joint possession is still illegal in most states, good grammar is always welcome.

○ ○ ○ ○ ○

How to pick the best first date movie

Sometimes I get tripped up by words so similar, they might as well be the same word. Take, for instance, the movies *The Illusionist* and *The Prestige*. Both came out in 2006. Both are about magicians. They should have only made one of them. This is how I also feel about the words *affect* and *effect*. Allow me to offer some ways to remember when to use each word correctly.

Affect starts with *a* which stands for *action*. An affect changes something. Usually, *affect* is a verb. I have never been affected by lackluster Ben Affleck flicks.[2] Movies have the potential to change us, however when you're cranking out duds like *Gigli* and *Daredevil,* the only thing being affected is my will to live. This is fun; I feel like I'm on *Mystery Science Theater 3000.* Maybe I should start a second column where I lampoon lousy movies from the 2000s.

Effect is the result of the affect's change. Usually, *effect* is a noun. Here's an example:

> The special effects in Nicolas Cage's portrayal of *Ghost Rider* made me want to take my face off.

Or how about:

> Side effects of watching Nicolas Cage's *Wicker Man* include massive disappointment and the feeling you'll never get those two hours of your life back.

Don't get me wrong—I love many Nic Cage films. He's acted in over 100 movies, and roughly 13 of them are fantastic.

Do you think you understand *affect/effect* now? Great. It's time for some exceptions (thanks, English). Occasionally, *affect* can be a noun and "effect" can be a verb. As a noun, *affect* means a feeling or emotional response. For example:

---

2   Be careful not to confuse the words "Affleck" and "affect."

When I watched *Fantastic Four* in theaters, my affect was upset and angry.

As a verb, *effect* means "to bring about." An example:

If you really want to effect change in America, build a time machine and tell them never to make the *Cats* movie.

Who knew you could learn grammar by reminiscing about movies you're too proud to admit you checked out from Blockbuster (back when that was a thing)? I actually kind of liked *Spiderman 3*; it had quite the affect on me.

○ ○ ○ ○ ○

Dating for math nerds

Is *none* singular or plural? If any mathletes out there are reading this, they would likely interject, "False! None is zero." And then they would adjust their adult retainers and get back to discussing their theories on who Rey's parents really are.

By choosing "is" in the sentence, the math nerds unwittingly made none singular, grammatically speaking. So does that mean zero equals one? No. I'm not about to anger the math community more than I already have.

When *none* means "not one" or "no part," use a singular verb. For example:

Because I wanted my body not to hate me, none of the McRib was eaten.

Similarly, *none* can be considered singular when part of a mass noun:

None of the wine was wasted.

Here, "wine" is a mass noun (as in: I drank the entire massive box of wine all by myself with some help from my trusty twisty straw.).

The plot now thickens quicker than a malted milkshake. While many believe "none" is always singular, *none* can also be plural. When you're able to substitute *none* for *not any,* *none* takes a plural verb. For instance:

> None of the members of the math club have ever kissed a girl.

> None of them were asked to the prom, so they held an alternative "prob," which is short for "probability." At the prob they thought their chances were statistically decent to end the night with a smooch from the cute girl who recently got contacts.

When you make *none* plural, it makes your syntax less awkward, just like Gwenifer (the girl with the contacts).

So, let's recap all of the *none* rules here. Use singular verb agreement when *none* quantifies a singular or mass noun. When *none* modifies a plural noun, to me, it sounds/reads better to use plural verb agreement, although both singular and plural are technically both acceptable. If someone suggests *none* always has to be singular, tell her it's none of her business. If that person is Gwenifer, try not to get lost in her suddenly unforgettable blue eyes.

What in the word?

Eek! is the noise you make when you see a mouse scurry through your kitchen.
Eke out is when you barely reach your goal
(to *eke out* a living or to *eke out* a victory).

Get over it

What? You're over me? When were you...under me?
—Ross Gellar, *Friends*

Don't return a phone call until at least 48 hours later. A man should have to pay for every date. Play hard to get. There's only one fish in the sea for each person. Online dating is just for nerds. These are all old rules of dating that aren't necessarily true or valid anymore. Does that mean I'm not romantic or chivalrous? That could be, but I prefer to consider myself "pragmatic."

Just like some dating rules seem either outdated or completely made up, we have at least a handful of grammar rules that mostly reflect antiquated guidelines written by a long-dead white guy. This isn't an attack on long-dead white guys, neither is it an assault on long-standing rules. There are many examples of dead white guys as well as old rules that we should still respect and admire.

One contentious rule that has changed (or at least devolved into about a dozen shades of gray) in the past decade is the usage of *more than* and *over*. I contend that the argument between *more than* and *over* isn't a clash of rules, but merely a difference in styles. According to the old "rule," use *more than* when you're talking about numbers:

> I watched more than 15 episodes of *The Good Place* in one sitting.

By the same "rule," the following sentence would be considered incorrect:

> I watched over 15 episodes of *The Good Place* in one sitting.

Even if you adhere to this long-standing guideline of grammar style, do you know why? William Cullen Bryant, a nineteenth-century poet and the editor of the *New York Evening*

Post, declared that this usage was his preferred style. Based on his editorial clout, other style and usage guides followed suit, including the AP Stylebook—until 2014.

When the good people who decide on the style guidelines for the AP Stylebook abandoned this rule, editors started an electronic Twitter riot with their outrage. This style change reflected an already popular usage in culture. While I'm sure editors around the country still twitch when they see *over* and *more than* used interchangeably, I appreciate the relaxing of this rule, which was basically someone's glorified preference from over a hundred years ago.

As in the rules of dating, rules of grammar change, as they should when culture and norms shift. The fact of the matter is that staying on top of your grammar game will help you succeed in your love life.

○ ○ ○ ○ ○

Cappuccino drinks are *not* made from Capuchin monkeys.

Have you ever been confused about something, but you didn't want to look dumb asking about it? For instance, you might think Cappuccino drinks are made from ground up Capuchin monkeys, even though that sounds pretty cruel. Without questioning the coffee industry, you just go along with it, until one day your girlfriend orders a Cappuccino during a date. Suddenly you shout at the top of your lungs, "How could you do that to the monkeys?!" in the middle of your local coffeehouse.

The words *presume* and *assume* are kind of like that. They're kind of similar, so let's just use them interchangeably. Wrong. I think to understand the difference between the two words, we need to understand what *-sume* means. Get your togas on, because it's time for a Latin lesson, folks!

According to *The Latin Dictionary, sumere* means "to put on or take up." Google's Latin to English translator sums it up in one word: take.

You already know that the prefix *pre-* means "before." So, when we presume something, we have "put on" what we think about something based on prior or previous knowledge or evidence. Presuming is when we suppose something based on a decent probability that it's true. For instance:

> When I walked into my lecture hall class, I presumed the woman in the pantsuit at the lectern was my professor.

The prefix *as-* shows up as a variant of the prefix *ad-* when the next letter in the word is an *s*. Trust me; I looked that up in the dictionary. The prefix *as-* means "assert." So *assume* is when we "assertively" "take" on an opinion about something without any evidence or prior knowledge. Assuming almost always gets us in trouble.

Both *presume* and *assume* have to do with "supposing" something. The difference is, presume is supposing something about which you already know at least a little bit. Think of *presume* as an educated guess and *assume* as an asinine guess.

To avoid looking asinine, get the facts on words like *presume* and *assume* before you use them in casual conversation. While you're at it, school yourself on common coffee terms; you'd hate to assume your significant other is a ground-up monkey-drinking psychopath.

○ ○ ○ ○ ○

Find some things you have in common

You only have to look as far as your social media feed to realize people disagree over just about everything in our current climate, including the assessment of our current climate. He's a crook! She's a liar! You're crazy! And that's among friends. It seems that the only thing we can agree on is we can't agree on anything.

In an effort to help us see eye to eye on something, let's discuss subject-verb agreement. Making mistakes on your subject-verb agreement is the quickest way to come across as a grammar amateur. A singular noun needs a singular verb to accompany it, and a plural noun takes a plural verb.

One of the easiest ways to get our subject and verb agreement crisscrossed is when other words or phrases come between them. Most of the time this comes in the form of prepositional phrases.

> This collection of presidential toenail clippings belongs in the Smithsonian.

In this sentence, "collection" is the subject and "belongs" is the verb. "Collection" is singular, as is "belongs." Don't be tempted to change the verb "belongs" to "belong" because of "toenail clippings," since "toenail clippings" is part of the prepositional phrase "of presidential toenail clippings."

When it comes to subjects that are indefinite pronouns, which include *someone, nobody, anything, each* and *either*; these words are all singular nouns. You can treat any of these indefinite pronouns just as you would *he, she,* and *it*. For example:

> Each of my pet porcupines hates broccoli.

The subject "each" is singular, so it takes the singular verb "hates." Like taking care of porcupines, these rules can prove prickly to master!

Finally, you've got to know what to do with all-too-common sneaky verbs like *have, do,* and *be*. Use "has" if your subject is a singular noun or a third-person singular pronoun: He has nineteen potatoes. If your subject is plural or is the pronoun *I, you, they* or *we*, use *have*:

I have only one potato; they have several.

In the same way, use *does* if your subject is a singular noun or a third-person singular pronoun:

She does goat yoga.

If your subject is plural or is the pronoun *I, you, they* or *we,* use *do.*

The verb *be* takes three different irregular forms in the present tense: *is, are,* and *am. Is* is singular; *are* is plural. Only use *am* with the pronoun *I.*

I think we can all agree that subject-verb agreement is complicated, but, if we all learn these grammar rules, we can all have something in common.

What in the word?

Exercise is what you do when you go to the gym.
Exorcise is what you do when you get rid of demons.

The art of the compliment

Humility is tricky. On the one hand, you don't want to look like a jerk by taking all the credit when the boss says, "Nice work on the executive Powerpoint presentation." On the other hand, the "aw, shucks" response when someone appreciates something about you says to the world "feel free to walk all over me." So, the question of the day is: how do you accept a compliment?

If you noticed, I just used the word *compliment* spelled with an *i.* What's the difference between *compliment* with an *i* and *complement* with an *e*? Let's get to the bottom of this absurd, misheard word duo.

A compliment merely is when someone says something nice about you. It's an expression of admiration or acclaim. "You have nice eyes." "I really like how you peeled those sweet potatoes." "You're the best underhanded free throw shooter on the whole basketball team." Those are all examples of compliments.

Complements are horses of a slightly different color. A complement is something that completes or perfects another thing. This is easy to remember because *complement* and *complete* look like similar words. When Forrest Gump told Jenny that they went together like peas and carrots, he was suggesting that Forrest and Jenny complement each other. Good wine pairings are examples of things that complement each other:

The '62 Cabernet complemented the filet mignon superbly.

There are several other examples of complementary categories, from math to music to color theory. Just remember that *complement* with an *e* looks like the word *complete*.

I think we worry that if we accept a compliment, we'll come across as conceited or full of ourselves. No one wants to have the reputation of being cocky. However, I believe that when someone compliments you, you simply look him in the eye and respond with a genuine "Thank you, I really appreciate that." Not only are you exuding a healthy level of confidence in your own skills, but you're accepting the gift that the complimenter is attempting to give you.

When you don't accept a compliment, it's almost like someone gives you a gift, you open it, look at it, shake your head, and give it back to the person. So, what I'm suggesting is that accepting a compliment from someone is the polite thing to do. It doesn't make you an arrogant jerk; it makes you gracious. Just remember to return the favor next time you notice something good in the other person.

○ ○ ○ ○ ○

How to know when the end is near

The worst words in the English language are, 'We have to talk.' Either that or, 'Whose bra is this?'
—*Jerry Seinfeld*

When your significant other starts a conversation with, "So, we need to talk," you know it's over. You immediately flip through the pages of your relationship, scanning for any glaring issues or things for which you should be sorry. You're on the defensive. You might even think about who gets to keep which friend after the impending break-up.

Some, perhaps many, people believe fervently it's not kosher to begin a sentence with *so*. I'm here to advocate for the use of *so* as an acceptable sentence starter. If this is a dealbreaker for the relationship between you and me, then I agree that it's time for us to start seeing other people.

So is a coordinating conjunction. This type of conjunction's prime purpose is to join other sentence elements that go together. In case you're wondering, it's easy to remember English's seven coordinating conjunctions: just remember "FANBOYS," as in "For, And, Nor, But, Or, Yet and So." So, if this type of conjunction joins related parts of a sentence, how is it acceptable to start a sentence with one? I thought you'd never ask.

According to the Chicago Manual of Style, "There is a widespread belief—one with no historical or grammatical foundation—that it is an error to begin a sentence with a conjunction such as and, but or so. In fact, a substantial percentage (often as many as 10 percent) of the sentences in first-rate writing begin with conjunctions. It has been so for centuries, and even the most conservative grammarians have followed this practice."

If your mind isn't blown yet, consider the famous last line of F. Scott Fitzgerald's *The Great Gatsby*: "So we beat on, boats against the current, borne back ceaselessly into the past." The fact is, as Chicago points out, we've been cool with starting sentences with prepositions for quite a long time. With *so*, we use it to mean thus, therefore, or accordingly.

While we could probably connect sentences that begin with *so* to prior sentences with semicolons to show the connection between the two thoughts, we don't need to do this in everyday speech. If you're addressing the U.N., maybe try to avoid starting a sentence with *so*. Otherwise, you have my permission to *so* away.

○ ○ ○ ○ ○

How to get dates right

Chivalry isn't dead...yet. Follow these tips to make sure your Valentine's date wants to smooch you into oblivion at the end of the night. After all, yours truly was quite the dating doyen prior to shifting my interests to grammar.

For instance, women love it when you open doors for them. They love it when you open jars for them. However, women don't like it when you open their mail and read it before they get home from work. They also aren't too happy when you open their medicine cabinets to check which prescriptions they're taking. Trust me.

Now that you're getting your dating life figured out, I want to tell you how to write dates properly. Perhaps your shortcomings in writing dates correctly are having an effect on whether or not you're getting romantic dates. It could be.

Anyway, according to the AP Stylebook, you should use figures for dates and years, and don't use *-st, -nd, -rd,* or *-th* with dates. So, you shouldn't write February 14th or February fourteenth; always write "February 14." You wouldn't write "Nineteen hundred and eighty-five" (although that's one of my favorite Wings songs); you should always write out 1985.

As if that weren't enough mind-blowing clarity on writing dates, I have more rules to lay on you. When it comes to months, they are always capitalized. The months of March, April, May

June and July should never be abbreviated, but you should abbreviate the remaining months when they're followed by a date (e.g., Feb. 14). The correct abbreviations for these months are Jan., Feb., Aug., Sept., Oct., Nov., and Dec.

Add -*s* (but no apostrophe) after numbers when you're writing decades or centuries (e.g., the 1900s). Do add an apostrophe when you're writing a decade if numerals are omitted (e.g., the '20s).

I'm going to throw this in because I'm sure you're wondering: the word February comes from a Roman festival of washing and purification (called Februa) that happened every spring. It was previously known as Lupercalia, which was a violent, sexually-charged fertility festival. In the late fifth century A.D., Pope Gelasius replaced this pagan holiday with St. Valentine's Day, which remembers the martyrdom of St. Valentine on February 14, 269.

If you want to speak the language of love to your sweetheart, make sure you know how to write dates the right way. Otherwise, the only dates you'll be getting are the kind that are less-good versions of raisins.

What in the word?

Elicit is when you evoke or bring out a response.
Illicit is something that is illegal (like using Comic Sans for anything other than a kid's birthday invitation).

At least pretend to care

I care approximately zero about owning a watch. I can't imagine (at this point where our phones rule our lives and do everything for us) ever needing to own a watch. I don't care about them as fashion accessories, neither do I need to have one as a status statement. After I take a watch off, my arm hairs all stand at attention as if the commander of the arm hair army is passing by.

So, should I say "I could care less about watches" or "I couldn't care less about watches?"

I should correctly say "I couldn't care less about watches." This implies that my level of caring about watches is already so low it may as well be nonexistent. It's not possible for me to care any less about owning a watch. Even nerdy calculator watches are redundant at this point unless you're wearing one ironically. And I don't really see the point in the smart watch.

With my smartphone, I have no need for a watch. As a man who wears male clothing, my pockets are big enough for my wallet, phone and Burt's Bees lip balm. Don't get me started on pockets and gender privilege. It's totally a thing. Men have an upper hand even when it comes to functional, amply-sized pockets.

When you say "I could care less," it implies that you can, in fact, care less. Unless you're using this phrase sarcastically, you're using it incorrectly. "I could care less about humans," the uppity housecat yawned to herself. First of all, that cat can talk! Secondly, she's implying that she has the capacity to care less about humans, even though she has not exhibited any evidence that she has ever cared about humanity (with the exception of when she's hungry).

Perhaps the key to reducing our anxiety and stress is to start caring less about things out of our control. We get so consistently worked up about the littlest things. On the other hand, maybe you couldn't care less about this entire topic. If that's the case, you're already ahead of your time.

○ ○ ○ ○ ○

If all else fails, just buy her a candle.

Never use abstract nouns when concrete ones will do. If you mean "More people died" don't say "Mortality rose." — C.S. Lewis, Letters to Children

Think about concrete for a second...even if you weren't already thinking about it. Can you picture it? Can you feel its hardness? Do you see a driveway, sidewalk, or building in your mind? Concrete is solid. I promise I'm not being paid by the big concrete lobby or anything (although I'd be open to laying the foundation for a strong relationship).

When we talk about *concrete* as a noun, we think about driveways. As an adjective, *concrete* is anything you can experience using your five senses; it's the opposite of abstract. Something that is abstract doesn't exist in material form. Right now we're tackling abstract and concrete nouns.

Remember how a noun is a person, place, thing, or idea? The first three are easy; they fall into the territory of concrete nouns. Only when we get into the "idea" category do things get dicey. Abstract nouns are things like freedom and love. You can't buy a scented version of an abstract noun at Yankee Candle.

I suppose you could buy a candle that smells like freshly poured concrete. Is concrete considered *cement* when it's wet and only becomes concrete when it hardens? Is it like magma and lava or bread and toast? These are the things that keep me up at night. You could obviously buy an apple pie or pumpkin spice candle. But you can't bottle *wisdom* or even taste *disappointment*. Try as they might, the scent scientists at the Yankee Candle laboratory couldn't candleize an abstract noun even if they burned the candle at both ends.

To help you remember abstract nouns, know that they fall into the following categories: feelings, states, emotions, qualities, concepts, ideas and events. This accounts for everything from stress to faith to democracy. I'd like to see those wax nerds try to put an abstract noun like *pessimism* into candle form.

Here are some concrete nouns you may think are abstract. Although untouchable, rainbows are concrete (you can see them). Even though it's invisible, noise is concrete (you can hear it). Is this starting to make sense?

The next time you play Mad Libs on a road trip, I dare you to use only abstract nouns in your game. Like abstract nouns, it will be full of total non-sense.

Become King of the Word Nerds

How good grammar will make you the coolest smart person in the history of the universe

Be nice to nerds. Chances are you'll end up working for one.
—Bill Gates

Nerds rule the world. Don't believe me? The top 10 wealthiest Americans, according to the 2019 *Forbes* list, includes two Microsoft CEOs, two Google founders, the founder of Oracle, the founder of Facebook, the founder of Amazon, and one bigtime newspaper nerd (I'm looking at you, Mr. Buffett.). True, these are all white dudes[1], but they're also nerds. That's what I'd like to focus on in this section. Do you want to become Scrooge McDuck-level wealthy? Invent something in your garage. Start an innovative website. But, what role does grammar play in nerds' global

---

1   I'll take "White Male Privilege" for $500.

dominance? Fair question.

In a 2016 PLOS ONE study, researchers found correlations between introverts and good grammar. Nerdy types tend to be introverted, although that's not true 100% of the time. I'm mostly speaking for myself here, as a nerd. Keep in mind: I have red hair and glasses. Stop to think about any TV show or movie with a red-headed person with glasses. Is that person in a heist movie, sitting inside an unmarked van behind a computer attempting to break into a remote computer mainframe? I thought so. Typecasting!

The aforementioned study, however, comes with a warning for grammar nerds: don't be a jerk! The researchers found a correlation between people who excel at grammar and high levels of judgmentalism. Perhaps that's a reason nerds like us have a harder time keeping and making friends; we're better with computers than we are with other people.

If you think about your grammar prowess as a lightsaber of truth, you have to try extra hard to stay on the light side of The Force. Don't go around hacking at everything like Darth Grammarius; if you do, you'll find yourself as the hopeless villain in an epic struggle for intergalactic justice. Proceed with caution. Wield your knowledge wisely.

○ ○ ○ ○ ○

Forget everything you know; our teachers lied to us.

Pluto isn't a planet. There's a fifth ocean. Math is different now. Davy Crockett didn't die defending the Alamo; he was captured and later executed. At least, we think so. It seems that facts are changeable. After all, anyone can log in and edit a Wikipedia entry... *(typing some stuff into my web browser)* ...voila! The Boston Tea Party actually happened in Scranton. This resulted in the infamous "Dunder Mifflin Fire," which Ryan started.

Our entire education was a lie!

Before we all get unnecessarily dramatic and say stuff we don't really mean, let's just acknowledge that textbooks don't always get things right. In fact, textbooks were kind of a new thing in the mid-1800s when the convenient rhyme "I before E except after C" gained popularity. Too bad this mnemonic device is wildly incorrect.

The full rhyme states, "I before E, except after C—or when sounded like A as in 'neighbor' and 'weigh.'"

But what about those foreign atheists who routinely seize caffeinated heifers? It doesn't take an Einstein to figure out this rule is just plain weird. I'm not going to leave your education in a heap of rubble; instead, I'm going to make it more complicated and rebuild it (and then remind you there are always exceptions to rules).

Here's a new rule for you that will handle most of your spelling conundrums: use *I* before *E* (*believe, priest, thief*) except when *C* is followed by *L, P, T* or *V* (*receipt, conceive, ceiling*), or when sounded like *A* as in weight or *I* as in height (*neighbor, sleigh, heist, height*), or when a prefix or suffix implies *E-I* (*reiterate, de-ionize, canoeing*).

Phew.

Unfortunately, even this long rule still has exceptions like either, forfeit, sovereign and reveille. Still, the rule I outline above works 99% of the time.

General Douglas Macarthur famously said, "Rules are mostly made to be broken and are too often for the lazy to hide behind." We won't judge the general too harshly for ending his sentence in a preposition; instead, we'll just consider how his words (if true even some of the time) make English spelling and grammar so tricky.

The only way to know how to spell all these words correctly is to memorize them. I recommend investing in a nice set of flashcards; you can study them during your leisure time.

○ ○ ○ ○ ○

Use Latin to impress people and be awesome.

I am sorry that I cannot address the people of
Latin America in their own language—Latin.
—Dan Quayle

You probably weren't surprised to learn I was an English major for one semester in college. I'm about to ratchet up the nerd factor and divulge another academic secret of mine: I took three years of Latin in high school. And, for a dead language, Latin is everywhere. Ever heard of an astronaut? They didn't have those back in the Roman Empire, but *astronaut* gets its name from combining the Latin word for star (*astrum*) with the word for sailor (*nauta*). Boom: star sailor.

We use Latin in our abbreviations all the time without really even knowing what they mean. Now I'm going to focus on *i.e.* and *e.g.* and try to help you understand when each is appropriate to use.

The abbreviation *i.e.* stands for *id est*, which is Latin for "that is." Use *i.e.* when you want to clarify or further define what you just stated. Think of *i.e.* as "in essence." Here's an example:

> Carmel's City Council recently removed funding for the mayor's $5 million carousel, i.e., one super-expensive horse tornado.

The abbreviation *e.g.* stands for *exempli gratia*, which means "for example" in Latin. It's easy to remember *e* is for "example." I like to think of *e.g.* as "egg sample," which would be a strange item to try on sample day at Sam's Club. Here's an example for you:

> I love any kind of fall activity (e.g., jumping in leaf piles, watching football, and consuming any pumpkin-flavored beverage).

Here are some other things to remember: always add periods after each letter in *i.e.* and *e.g.* They are abbreviations, not their own words. Always add a comma after the abbreviations, even if your spell check interjects a squiggly red line beneath it.

Other Latin abbreviations that are part of our everyday lives include *R.I.P., P.S., C.V., N.B., per cent.,* and *vs.* They are all ticked they didn't get any attention in this book, i.e., not the prettiest ponies at the petting zoo.

○ ○ ○ ○ ○

How to best utilize your time at the library

As I write this, I'm sitting by myself. For those of you who love being alone in total silence, let me let you in on an introvert pro tip: hang out in the periodical room at your local library. You'll either be alone or with (at most) three other people reading today's newspaper (because they were too cheap to pay for a subscription).

I enjoy being by myself. But the word *myself* gets misused more and more as a result of well-meaning people who are un-knowingly over-correcting their grammar.

Here's an example I hear often:

If you still haven't found what you're looking for, feel free to call Adam, Larry or myself.

How would you write this without Adam or Larry in the sentence? You wouldn't say "..feel free to call myself;" you'd say "...feel free to call me." Now, if you throw back in Adam and Larry, this doesn't change.

If you still haven't found what you're looking for, feel free to call Adam, Larry or me.

You see, *myself* is a reflexive pronoun. Others include *your-self, herself, himself* and *itself.* These words are never subjects of a sentence; they're always objects. If you want a good way to re-member this, think about when you look down to gaze deeply into the water of a placid pond and you see your reflection in it. Your inner dialogue would say something like, "I see myself in the water." In the same way you see a reflection of yourself in the water, words like *yourself* are reflexive pronouns.

Other than using "myself" as an object, when should you use *myself*? Use *myself* when you are both the subject and the object of the same sentence:

> I can see myself spending more time hanging out in the periodical room.

Here you're the object of your own action.
You should also use *myself* to add emphasis to a statement:

> I myself locked the door so no one else could get in.

Or how about:

> I wrote this all by myself.

In both these sentences, you could omit myself and the sentence would still make sense; using *myself* in these cases adds a dramatic flair.

I encourage you to spend some time to be by yourself; hopefully you'll enjoy the company.

What in the word?

Bail is when you post money to get out of jail. It's also what you do when you flake out on your friends at the last minute.
Bale is a large bundle of something, like mail or hay.
Christian Bale is the best Batman. End of discussion.

Lessons from *Lord of the Rings*

Let's think about *Lord of the Rings* for a minute (and all word nerds rejoiced!). Remember Sméagol/Gollum? Whether you read Tolkien's three-part epic or you watched it on the big screen (or both), Sméagol is an unforgettable character. He can turn from endearing and sweet to greedy and vengeful within the same breath. Today we're going to look at the verbal equivalent of Sméagol: contranyms.

A contranym is a word that has multiple meanings, one of which is diametrically opposed to another. Contranyms are also known as antagonyms or autoantonyms. If we're on an epic quest to destroy a magical super-ring (in this case, the super-ring is bad grammar), we have to watch out for contranyms (a.k.a. verbal Sméagols) along the way so we don't veer off the path of syntactic truth.

Here's an example of a contranym: *left*. Left can mean either "departed" or "remaining." Depending on your sentence, you could end up left in the dark (see what I did there?). If Frodo leaves the other Hobbits to go back to the Shire, who's left? Depending on your definition of *left*, the answer is either Frodo or the other Hobbits. Sneaky little Hobbits!

Throw out is another tricky contranym. It could either mean to dispose of or to present for consideration. In the case of our Hobbit friends in their journey to destroy the "one ring to rule them all," *throw out* could change the outcome of the story depending on how it's used. On one hand, the Hobbits could throw out (dispose of) the ring into the molten lava of Mount Doom, thus fulfilling their mission. Alternatively, what if Sam threw out (presented for consideration) an idea in which the group of Hobbit friends instead kept the ring so they could turn invisible whenever they wanted to sack Gandalf's firework collection? Contranyms can really change the story.

I can think of an array of other contranyms. Some include *dust, oversight, custom, buckle, bolt, refrain* and *trim*.

We're probably much more familiar with synonyms, homonyms and antonyms. When we stumble on such a unique type of word like a contranym, it really can become something precious—just like the One Ring.

○ ○ ○ ○ ○

How to capitalize on being a word nerd

I'm about to hit you with a mnemonic device that will bring the armies of men into peace with the wood elves. That's right, I have one device to rule them all when it comes to remembering the eight rules of capitalization, and it comes from *Lord of the Rings*. Is this going to be nerdy? You betcha. Are you ready? Whenever you want to recall what gets capitalized, just remember "Forgetful Bilbo Baggins took Pippin into Sam's watermelon marmalade store." It's as simple as that.

F is for the *first letter* in a sentence. This is an easy one. Always capitalize the first letter in a sentence. Your phone automatically does it, as does your computer's word processing software. That's why God invented Clippy.

B stands for *buildings* and other manmade structures. This means we need to capitalize the Statue of Liberty, the Eiffel Tower and the Brooklyn Bridge.

The second *B* is for *borders* of countries, states, counties and regions. Always capitalize Jamaica, New Jersey, Jakarta and Jefferson County.

T is for *titles*. This relates to people (Doctor Quinn), jobs (when the job title immediately precedes the person's name: Author Tom Clancy), and book and movie titles (*The Hunt for Red October*). You'll notice I didn't capitalize "for" in the previous title. In titles, do capitalize the first word, adjectives, nouns and the last word. Do not capitalize conjunctions (including and, but and or), articles (a, an, the) or prepositions (including for, to or by).

P is for *people*. Always capitalize people's names (Frodo, Sauron, Gandalf, etc.).

I is for *I*. Yes, an I for an I. Capitalize the word *I*. Again, many of our robot devices do this for us automatically. Also, make sure never to stare directly into the Eye of Sauron; it will haunt your dreams for one thousand eternities.

S is for *schools*, including colleges and universities. Although I don't think Gandalf ever taught at Hogwarts School of Witchcraft and Wizardry, I'm sure they'd let him substitute.

W is for bodies of *water*. The Red River separates Oklahoma from Texas. The Southern Ocean wasn't a thing when I was in school. You get the idea.

M is for *mountains*. Be careful when climbing Mount Doom; you might drop your jewelry into it.

Finally, *S* is for *streets*. Good luck finding a place where the streets have no name, because people love naming things. The president lives at 1600 Pennsylvania Avenue. Although The Beatles sang about Penny Lane, their recording studio was on Abbey Road.

Forgetful Bilbo Baggins took Pippin into Sam's watermelon marmalade store. Memorize that and you'll be able to harness all the powers of capitalization against the terrible gaze of the Eye of Sauron.

○ ○ ○ ○ ○

There's an underground Mount Doom in Yellowstone Park.

I'm totally qualified to warn you about this next subject. Not only is my brother-in-law a meteorologist, but I took a course called *Volcanoes and Earthquakes* in college. It was an online course. I took it to satisfy my non-lab science class. I only had to show up to take tests. I needed a 90% or better to bring my final letter grade up to a C. I got a *C* in *Volcanoes and Earthquakes* (online). Therefore, since I passed the class, I'm going to pass on a bit of foreboding news to you.

You may want to sit down for this.

There's a supervolcano under Yellowstone National Park called the Yellowstone Caldera that last erupted in a big way approximately 640,000 years ago. The next time it erupts, it could potentially result in a large swath of North America getting covered in ash, creating a sustained volcanic winter that kills roughly half the world's population. Now, before we get ahead of ourselves, scientists at the Yellowstone Volcano Observatory warn against overreacting to reports that this supervolcano is overdue for another full-scale eruption. In fact, they reassure us that "recurrence intervals of these events are neither regular nor predictable."

Oh, good. The dormant supervolcano is unpredictable. Let's not anger it.

Okay, let's set aside the looming volcano apocalypse to talk about the words "sit" and "set." These two are easily confused and often get mistakenly interchanged.

Set means to "put something in a specific place." *Set* is (almost always) a transitive verb. Transitive verbs are always action verbs and they always require direct objects. Direct objects act on another noun. Take the following sentence:

> We should set aside our differences; the big volcano could erupt at any time.

"We" is the subject. "Set" is the transitive verb. "Differences" is the direct object.

Sit means "to be seated." *Sit* is an intransitive verb. Intransitive verbs are always action verbs and they do not require direct objects. Consider this example:

> You shouldn't sit there; the supervolcano is directly beneath your feet!

In the first complete thought before the semicolon, "you" is the subject and "sit" is the intransitive verb. The sentence has no direct object.

Set requires another thing to make sense. For instance, you can set secret Oreos on top of the cabinet so your kids don't know about them. You can set your keys on the table. When you sit, you sit yourself and nothing else. I sit. She sits. Banjo the trained sloth sits on the top of the giant cheese sculpture. The supervolcano sits and waits to wreak havoc on planet Earth. You get the idea.

Whether or not the Yellowstone Caldera decides to usher in the end of humanity, it's a good idea to understand the difference between *sit* and *set*. Although I doubt the world depends on it, it's possible our future lava overlords will give us a pop quiz on the difference between the two. Depending on which version of the multiverse we inhabit presently, having a solid handle on *sit* and *set* could save us from total destruction.

What in the word?

A *travesty* is a mocking or distorted portrayal of something, often comical.
A *tragedy* is a disastrous event, serious in nature.

If volcanos don't kill us, the robots will.

There is no future. Feel free to go back to bed now.

You probably think I'm referring to the fact that we recently took a picture of a black hole, or maybe that climate change is happening at such a rapid pace it seems as if our planet is a lost cause. Or maybe you're concerned about who is (or isn't) in elected office, pervasive hatred, ongoing inequality, the increased loneliness indirectly caused by technology, or that, in any movie about robots that takes place in the future, robots inevitably destroy humanity. It doesn't take a flux capacitor to realize that the future depends on our present actions.

Whoa, that's tense.

Actually, I don't want to talk about the future today. I'd like to discuss the future tense, which, in English, technically doesn't exist. According to Bas Aarts (which I promise isn't a name I invented by throwing random Scrabble tiles on the ground), author of *Oxford Modern English Grammar,* "English has no future tense, because it has no future tense inflections, in the way that many other languages do, nor any other grammatical form or combination of forms that can exclusively be called a future tense."

When we learn Latin, Spanish, or French in high school, we learn all the first, second and third person verb conjugations in past, present, and future tense inflections. English only has one way to express tense with inflections (word endings), and that's in the past tense. When we add *-ed* to a verb like *punt,* it becomes a past tense verb. I punted the ball onto my neighbor's roof. We have no future inflections in English.

What about *will?* I knew you'd ask. In a sentence like "I will go to the gym tomorrow," *will* serves as a modal verb, which is an auxiliary verb that expresses necessity or possibility. Other modal verbs are words such as *shall, can, may,* and *could.*

In grammar, there's an important distinction between tense and time. Tense is a grammatical term that is directly tied to a verb's inflection. Time is a human construct on which we base our reality. In that construct, we have three times: the past, present, and future. When we use *will* with a verb, we are expressing future time, but we are not technically making something future tense.

If you ask me, it won't be the future until our flying cars are powered by trash. So, until then, I'm sending good grammar wishes to all my fellow word nerds.

...also vampires.

If you had a time machine to go back and re-do one moment of your life, what would you change? For me, I would learn where to place the word *only* in a sentence properly. This grammar faux pas of mine doesn't get past you word nerds out there. In fact, I've received at least seven emails about my misplacement of *only* over the past few months. So, if you don't mind, I'm going to learn my lesson once and for all; after all, yours truly should get this right (lest readers think me a dullard).

Only is like a key fob with weak batteries—it's effective just when it's as close to the thing it's modifying as possible. So, when you move *only* around in a sentence, it gunks up or completely changes the meaning of your sentence. The proximity of *only* to the word or phrase it modifies is crucial.

The more I look at the word *only,* the more it reminds me of the way we use the word *just.* In these examples, when you see *only,* substitute it in your mind with the word *just.*

Only vampires bite humans in the neck. This sentence implies that no one besides vampires bites humans in the neck area.

Vampires bite humans only in the neck. Here, the implication is that vampires don't bite humans anywhere else. Here's a quick public service announcement: if you're thinking about getting a neck tattoo, don't.

Vampires only bite humans in the neck. This use of *only* implies that vampires don't do anything else to humans except bite their necks. Vampires don't pick humans' noses, they don't style humans' hair, and they don't jiggle the loose skin on humans' upper arms.

Vampires bite only humans in the neck. This suggests vampires don't bite ostriches, giraffes, flamingos, or anything else in the neck—just humans.

Only vampires bite humans in the neck.

Vampires *only* bite humans in the neck.

Vampires bite *only* humans in the neck.

Vampires bite humans *only* in the neck.

Placement of the word *only* changes the meaning of each sentence. Maybe it's time to stock up on turtlenecks.

Apparently, I understand grammar best when I use nerdy examples like vampires and time machines. And, now that I've learned my lesson, I can save my single-use time machine do-over for something else, such as the time I attempted to iron my shirt while still wearing it.

○ ○ ○ ○ ○

Vampires and werewolves can get along.

At Halloween time, kids in costumes aren't the only spooky things in the neighborhood. Did you know commas can save innocent lives? I wanted to avoid controversial subjects like killing in this column, but here we are discussing the only two certainties in life: death and punctuation.

I'm about to settle the Oxford comma debate once and for all. How's that for a bold statement?

Suppose I wanted to list a few (three, to be precise) of my favorite things. I could say: I like eating, children and small animals. That was intended to read as a list of three things, not a list of one thing followed by examples (although I've heard squirrel bacon is excellent)! Most people think the Oxford comma (a.k.a. the serial, series or Harvard comma) is at odds with the AP Stylebook. I'm not sure if this will come as a trick or a treat to you, but the AP Stylebook actually makes clear that it's perfectly appropriate to use an Oxford comma when doing so helps to avoid confusion or misinterpretation.

My general rule is: use commas sparingly. Pretend they're shotgun shells and you're trying to survive in a zombie apocalypse. According to AP, "If a comma doesn't help make clear what is being said, don't use it."

> I love secretly eating my child's Skittles, Milky Ways and Butterfingers once he's asleep.

In my opinion, this sentence doesn't need a comma after "Milky Ways" because it doesn't provide further clarity in the sentence's meaning, neither does it lead to misinterpretation.

Hopefully this nuanced take on the comma controversy provides a diacritical middle ground for the two feuding punctuation parties. I'm not naive enough to assume I will be able to change anyone's mind on a polarizing topic such as this; I merely wanted to illustrate how two opposing factions can (theoretically) peacefully coexist. I know, I know—you probably think this is a not-so-subtle way of addressing the age-old rivalry between vampires and werewolves. For the record, you are correct. I believe in a world in which vampires and werewolves can (and do) get along.

○ ○ ○ ○ ○

Snakes on a plank

I think we can solve many of life's problems by playing out theoretical battles between the opposing groups. For instance, when someone decides to make his March Madness picks based on theoretical mascot matchups, he usually ends up with the Michigan State Spartans as the tournament champions. This isn't a bad pick; the Spartans are a perennial Final Four team.

How about werewolves against vampires? Do bears beat *Battlestar Galactica*? Hufflepuff or Gryffindor? DC versus Marvel? There are so many good matchups to entertain.

In this case, we need to think about snakes versus pirates. Why in the world do we need to play out this battle? First of all, I know my friend Byron is going to read this and he hates snakes, but his favorite baseball team is the Pittsburgh Pirates. Secondly, we can clear up a big grammar gaffe by thinking about pirates and snakes. It's time to talk about *there is* and *there are*.

Increasingly I've heard people throwing around *there is* or *there's* when they ought to say "there are." Does this matter? Of course! After all, singular subjects need singular verbs; likewise, plural subjects get plural verbs. This is called subject-verb agreement.

However, with a subject like *there*, how do we know if the subject is singular or plural? Let's use an example:

> There is/are many ways to get to this afternoon's drum circle.

But, wait a second: "there" can't possibly be the subject, can it? No, it's not. In fact, the subject is "ways," although it's not clear when we're beginning the sentence.

Think of it this way: there are = pirates. Pirates say, "ARRRRR!" There is = snake. A snake says, "HISSSS!" One snake is singular. Multiple pirates are plural. Let's substitute "there" with "snake" and then "pirates" into our sentence: Snake is many ways to get to this afternoon's drum circle. Pirates are many ways to get to this afternoon's drum circle. Although they both sound ridiculous, "pirates" sounds better.

Here's another way to figure out which verb to take: turn it into a question.

> Is/are there many ways to get to this afternoon's drum circle?

In this case, you would rightly say, "Are there many ways to get to this afternoon's drum circle?"

A snake (which goes HISSSS!) is singular. Pirates (who go ARRRRR!) are plural. There is = singular. There are = plural. In a battle between one snake and a crew of pirates, I'd put my doubloons on the pirates; one snake couldn't possibly take a whole pirate posse down. Pirates beat snakes. There's plenty of room for argument here.

What in the word?

Awe is a feeling of respectful wonder.
Aww is what you say when you see a cuddly kitten.

Science has gone too far.

Somewhere in a secret laboratory (probably in Minsk), a team of thermodynamic scientists worked for years to perfect the to-go mug that hermetically traps heat, keeping your coffee or tea hot for hours. They traded handshakes and perhaps a few high fives before scalding their taste buds on some celebratory hot chocolate. It was certainly a historic occasion in the field of drink container science.

My biggest question isn't a grammar question. I want to know: just how long do we need to keep our drinks hot? Is it that important for our coffee to stay at near-boiling temperatures for up to six hours? I think the whole industry needs to cool off a bit.

Now here's my grammar question: should you write/say *a historic* or *an historic*? Let's dive in.

When you think about world-changing events like the moon landing, the signing of the Declaration of Independence, or the cup scientists perfecting a heat-sealing tumbler, you probably imagine someone referring to any of these as *an historic* occasion. Technically, this isn't correct! So, what's the rule?

Use the article *an* when it precedes any word that starts with a vowel sound. This certainly applies to words that begin with a silent *h*, including heir, honor and hour. It doesn't apply to words in which you pronounce the *h* sound, such as *heroic, hysterical* or *historic*. So, why do people put *an* in front of those words? Probably because at some point back in England people dropped the *h* sound in these words and supplied *an* before them (to properly imagine this, I hear someone speaking in a thick Cockney accent). The article *an* hung on although people started to uniformly pronounce the *h* sound in these words.

Old habits die hard, as when I take a swig of my morning tea too early, even though I know it's still way too hot. Either people still add *an* before words like historic because they learned to say it that way from previous generations, or they're just snooty. There's a fancy term for speech or writing that is only designed to impress: it's called an affectation. For most people, they probably add *an* because that's how they've always heard it pronounced. For people who prefer to be snooty, I heard there's a great sale at the monocle store: all glasses are half off.

○ ○ ○ ○ ○

Give Geoff Chaucer a chance.

I could write a whole section on *who*. *Who* or *whom*. *Who's* vs. *whose*. Who's on first? Who let the dogs out? Who's the boss? From my best research, I've concluded *who* is either the name of a band who likes to sing about pinball or the guy who plays first base.

Just kidding. As a general rule, use *who* when you're referring to a person and *that* when you're referring to an object. Case closed.

I wish it were that easy. However, according to style guides including Chicago Manual of Style and Merriam-Webster Dictionary of English Usage, *who* and *that* can indeed be used interchangeably. Additionally, authors including Shakespeare,

Chaucer, and books such as the King James Bible often utilized *that* to refer to a person. I'm not about to argue with the Bible.

Since I'm not going to pick a fight with Bill Shakespeare and Geoff Chaucer, I'll let the Oxford English Dictionary do it for me. According to Oxford, you should always use *who* when referring to people and *that* when referring to an object. As English is an ever-evolving language, you can either be frustrated that English word usage is often a matter of opinion, or you can geek out on it like yours truly. To me, in twenty-first century English usage, *who* vs. *that* is a matter of dignity.

If you're referring to a person, I prefer to use *who*:

Bill is the guy who lives down the street.

Bill isn't a *that*; Bill is a *who*. Now, if you'd like to extend this rule to animals and pets (not that you asked), I think it depends how much you love your pet.

To revisit British rock icons The Who, they sing "Who are you? Who? Who? Who? Who?", not "That are you? That? That? That? That?" And I'm not about to pick a fight with Pete Townshend.

○ ○ ○ ○ ○

Shakespeare knew what he was talking about.

The following is a scenario based on real events. Any names have been changed to avoid embarrassment and grammar-shaming.

My friend, Ann, drives a van. Ann drives a tan van, and she's married to Stan, but this story isn't about him. It's about Ann and her tan van. One day, Ann's tan van was uncommonly tawny in its hue because, you see, it was dirty. "My van needs washed," surmised Ann.

As soon as Ann said this, my ears felt as if they were going to explode. I resisted the urge to correct her, because we were with a group of people, and I try to avoid correcting people's grammar in public.

If Prince Hamlet wondered "To be, or not to be, that is the question," then my question is: what happened to *to be*? You see, Ann's tan van needed to be washed. It didn't "need washed," as she declared. In this case, "washed" is what's considered a passive participle, and it requires the infinitive phrase *to be* in order to pass grammar muster.

I know this omission of *to be* doesn't happen only in Indiana; this may simply be a Midwestern grammar faux pas. I'm interested to see if readers from outside the Midwest hear this ear-splitting construction. If not, send me an email with your regional grammar issue.

Besides *need,* I've also heard this phraseology used with the words *want* and *like.* For instance: My pet bear wants scratched. My son likes fed multiple times per day. As I type this, my word processor's squiggly red line is having a field day. My pet bear wants to be scratched. My son likes to be fed multiple times per day.

I'm not sure what caused the omission of *to be.* Maybe high school students don't appreciate being forced to read Shakespeare in their English classes, so they've begun a rebellion and have answered Prince Hamlet with a resounding "not to be."

When Shakespeare wrote his plays, he wrote many of his jokes for the broadest audience possible. Now his stuff is considered "classic" and "timeless." Perhaps there's hope for my writing to stand the test of time after all. Of course, much of it still needs to be edited.

What in the word?

A *gambit* is a strategic maneuver.
A *gamut* is a full range or extent.

How to become a Jedi master at grammar

Does that title make sense? To be honest, it makes more sense than starting a movie series with the fourth movie. It's as if Yoda were in charge of numbering the movies or something. "Four, five, six, we start with. Then, one, two, three, sounds good to me, it does. Finally, seven, eight, nine, we should end with."

The Jedi[2] can be either good, bad or neutral? When do the Vulcans battle the Wookies? How is having a laser sword better than having a laser gun? What about laser tag?

I'll have to admit—I don't know much about *Star Wars*. Somehow I missed the window to watch them during my formative years. Although I have glasses, write about grammar and prefer staying inside, my lack of *Star Wars* appreciation makes others seriously second-guess my nerd street cred.

Here's what I do know about *Star Wars*: Luke and Leia were brother and sister, which made things awkward, especially after they kissed. Darth Vader was Luke's dad. We pretend *Episode I* never happened (especially Jar Jar). Han shot first. What shot second. And I don't know is on third. Also, Yoda is an awesome green Muppet (voiced by Frank Oz, who also who voiced Miss Piggy, Fozzie Bear, Cookie Monster, Bert and Animal, to name a few) who could go toe-to-toe with Chuck Norris in a head-to-head matchup.

But is Yoda's grammar correct? His sentence structure is certainly odd. He says things such as, "When nine hundred years old you reach, look as good you will not."

Odd, that sounds. Writing like this, I don't know why I am.

For the most part, English syntax (how we arrange our words) follows the same pattern. In order for a sentence to be complete, it needs a subject and a predicate. The predicate always includes a verb and often includes an object.

Most English sentences follow the subject-verb-object order.

2   The plural of Jedi is Jedi.

In one of these popular laser sword space movies, according to Google, Darth Vader says, "I find your lack of faith disturbing." In this sentence, "I" is the subject, "find" is the verb, and "lack of faith" is the object. Many other *Star Wars* quotes follow this subject-verb-object pattern. "I am your father." "I think I just blasted it." "Women always figure out the truth. Always."

Yoda's syntax follows a distinctly different pattern. For the most part, his sentences follow the object-subject-verb pattern. This pattern is only found in 0.3% of the world's languages. Let's take this quote from Yoda:

> Patience you must have, my young Padowan.

In this sentence, "patience" appears first, serving as the object. This is followed by "you", the sentence's subject. Finally, we get the verb, "have." Object-subject-verb. Here's another:

> Through The Force, things (object) you (subject) will see (verb).

Therefore, the answer to the question is: yes, Yoda's speech pattern is grammatically correct; strange to our ears, it just sounds.

What in the word?

Reckless is when someone is being completely careless, usually in a dangerous way.
Wreckless is not a word.

Live long and grammar.

And all dared to brave unknown terrors, to do mighty deeds, to boldly split infinitives that no man had split before—and thus was the Empire forged.
— Douglas Adams, The Hitchhiker's Guide to the Galaxy

When I started working at a new company, I was disappointed to learn that an "enterprise" account had absolutely nothing to do with voyaging spaceships. Instead, enterprise accounts are the "big fish" your team reels in so that your proverbial corporate boat stays afloat.

I hate to critique Captain Kirk, but when he utters "to boldly go where no man has gone before," he's technically breaking a grammar rule. Or is he? I know William Shatner (who famously played Captain James T. Kirk) is Canadian; does that hamper his grasp on correct English grammar?

"To boldly go" is an example of a split infinitive. Up until now, the only thing I was worried about splitting was my pants. So, what's an infinitive, anyway?

An infinitive is almost always a two-word verb phrase with the word *to* in front of the verb. Examples of infinitives include *to sneeze, to cry, to dance* and *to fail.*

A split infinitive occurs when you put an adverb between *to* and the verb. It's as if the adverb is rudely cutting in on you and your date at the prom, which makes you want to take the adverb out to the parking lot and punch it in the throat. Examples of split infinitives include *to loudly sneeze, to softly cry, to confidently dance* and *to utterly fail.*

So, what's the big deal? Are split infinitives a definitive no-no in English? Not necessarily.

The anti-split infinitive movement grew from a handful of prominent English grammarians in the eighteenth and nineteenth centuries who had nothing better to do than to try to bend popular opinions on English grammar rules to those of Latin. By now, these grammarians are all dead, so they don't get a say anymore.

With that said, it's probably a good idea to avoid split infinitives in your formal writing; many still view split infinitives as at least quasi-incorrect grammar usage. But, could you imagine the introduction of a classic show like *Star Trek* where Kirk says "...to go boldly where no man has gone before"? Pop (and nerd) culture just wouldn't be the same. I'll split with the grammar snobs and cling on to the Trekkers on this one.[3]

The big question you may be asking yourself is: who has better grammar—*Star Wars* or *Star Trek* fans? Believe it or not, I can answer this one for you. *Star Trek* fans are better grammarians.

Grammarly studied nearly 2,000 fan comments on both the *Star Trek* and *Star Wars* Reddit fan communities. According to the data, Trekkers have a 98.2% grammatical accuracy, while *Star Wars* fans have an accuracy score of 94.6%. Jedi devotees' largest gaffes involve punctuation while Klingon supporters suffer most from grammar errors. Does that make one franchise better than the other? I'll let the respective devotees continue to duke it out with their lightsabers and pointy ears. I've never really gotten into any of the "Star" movies. One sun is plenty for this pasty coppertop to deal with, so please don't beat me up because I don't care about "beam me up."

○ ○ ○ ○ ○

Virtual realty

Here's a fun fact about redheads: we produce our own vitamin D. This means winter's long nights and cloudy days don't have much effect on my melanin-challenged body. Because of this, I don't get too excited about the transition from winter to spring. There are some positive side effects of being a mutant.

---

3 So, I learned this the hard way, but *Star Trek* fans find it offensive to be called "Trekkies"; instead, they prefer the collective "Trekkers." Potato, tomato.

I can take or leave spring. The bugs come back, allergies emerge from hibernation, and "for sale" signs in front yards become as plentiful as dandelions. If this were a cartoon, all my Realtor friends would have cash register "ka-ching" sounds going off while dollar signs appeared in their puffy, pollen-plagued eyes.

Yes, spring is the season for house-selling, and, as someone who has watched enough *House Hunters* to consider himself a semi-professional Realtor, it's time to revisit some commonly confused words: realty and reality.

Let's go ahead and get this out of the way: *Realtor* does not have an invisible letter *i* hiding in the middle of it. I can't tell you how many times I hear people say "real-i-tor." There's no *i* in *Realtor*.

Realty is a noun that simply means real estate. Realty deals with the buying and selling of property (buildings and land).

Reality is the opposite of fiction. It is usually a noun that means "something real." As an adjective, it often modifies the word television: reality television. The irony isn't lost on me that reality TV claims to document "real" life, but it often is more produced than a soap opera.

That means shows like *House Hunters* could be considered realty reality TV. While that's a funny phrase, *House Hunters* is about as real as the Tooth Fairy. Many couples who appear on the show already have houses under contract prior to filming, and the rest of them are quite far along in the house-buying process. That's just the tip of the unrealistic iceberg when it comes to everyone's favorite show to watch while settling into a cozy couch coma on a Tuesday night.

When it comes to the word *Realtor,* why is it sometimes capitalized (like in this article, for instance)? A capital *R* Realtor is someone who is officially a member of the National Association of Realtors. *Realtor* is actually a trademarked term by the NAR, therefore many stylebooks (including the AP) encourage you to capitalize it and use it only if you're confident the person to whom you're referring is truly a capital *R* Realtor. If not, they advise, use the term *real estate agent* or *real estate broker*.

Even though I have to get all hopped up on Zyrtec, I actually do love spring. I also love *House Hunters* (especially *House Hunters International*) even though I know it's heavily staged. An entertaining reality TV show is nothing at which to sneeze.

○ ○ ○ ○ ○

Somehow William Hung made it into this book.

Do you remember William Hung? He auditioned for *American Idol* back in 2004 and became famous for how delightfully bad his performance was. Hung's version of Ricky Martin's "She Bangs" for the judges was so bad, it actually endeared him to fans. As a result, Hung had fifteen seconds of fame performing the equivalent of lousy karaoke on various television shows.

That's not the type of *hung* I want to tackle right now. It's time to discuss *hang, hung* and *hanged*. This tricky trifecta trips up the best of us. Let's get it straight, shall we?

Hang is a present tense verb with a handful of meanings. It means to fasten, to let droop, to pay close attention, or attach tightly to something. It's also an informal term for spending time with friends. Hang your coat on the hook. Hang out with the wrong crowd, and you'll end up in jail. I like to hang from the monkey bars. I'm hanging by a moment here with you. You don't really need me, but you keep me hanging on. Yes, those last two examples were song lyrics.

Hung, on the other hand, is the past tense form of *hang*. Almost always, *hung* is the proper past tense version of *hang* to use in your everyday vocabulary. William hung the curtains. We hung onto every second of William's terrible audition. As a result, Hung hung out with other D-list celebrities. The public hung William out to dry after his novelty act wore off.

When it comes to *hanged*, we need to be careful. It is the past tense and past participle of *hang* and should only be used when you're talking in the past tense about a person who got put to death via hanging. According to the AP Stylebook, "One hangs a picture, a criminal or oneself. Use hanged for executions or suicides; use hung for other actions." That's clear enough for me!

Remember it this way: curtains are hung and outlaws are hanged. I could keep talking about *hang, hung* and *hanged,* but my stomach is starting to growl at me. I'm going to wrap it up because when I have to wait too long for meals, I get hangry, and you won't like me when I'm hangry!

What in the word?

Flair is when you have a talent for something.
Flare is a rapidly burning torch.

The next to last word

If a potato can become vodka, then you can become a bonafide word nerd. The tools and tips I give you are meant to be used for good; please don't flaunt your grammar greatness over anyone, rather use it to lift everyone up. I'm about to share a word with you that will make everyone at the white-tie optional gala assume you're the king or queen of some distant, exotic land. Use this word and upper-crusters will begin consulting with you before they order their newest monocle. They'll picture you eating peeled champagne grapes while you brush the golden mane of your award-winning miniature pony named Lord Anponio.

I'm talking about the word *penultimate*. Although this sounds like a million-dollar word, it simply means "next to last" or "second to last." It's as simple as that. So, if you ate the "penultimate Oreo," that would mean you ate the next to last Oreo in the package. If you are reading the nineteenth chapter in a twenty-chapter book, you are reading the book's penultimate chapter. If you use the penultimate square of toilet paper, it's time to install a new roll so the next person isn't stuck with one lonely square.

Allow me to put on my horn-rimmed grammar nerd glasses for a second. The term *penult* is a noun that means the next to last syllable in a word. The penult in the word *automobile* is *mo*. Now you know that!

Certainly I'm not going to up the ante and share an even nerdier-yet-related word, am I?

Yes, I am: *antepenultimate*, which refers to the third to last item in a series, or the next to next to last thing. Going back to our twenty-chapter book: If chapter nineteen is the penultimate chapter, that means chapter eighteen is the antepenultimate chapter. If we break down the Latin meanings for each part of the word, we'd get "before" (*ante*) "almost" (*pen*) and "last" (*ultimate*). Antepenultimate is the thing that comes before the almost last thing.

Drop any of these words into casual conversation and your friends will offer you the finest bottle out of their wine cellars. *Horse & Hound* magazine (my favorite magazine about both dogs and horses) will call to request an in-depth interview about your dressage training techniques. Yes, my friends: if the humble potato can become vodka, then you too can achieve the high status of grammar guru. I believe in you. It's time to go out there and dominate the English language.

○ ○ ○ ○ ○

Ending with an interrobang

We're living in the golden age of outrage. If you're just finishing a three-year social media cleanse, I've got some bad news for you: people are ticked off.

People are royally ticked about pretty much everything:

guns, kneeling, not kneeling, walls, refugees, Starbucks (in general), and anything that remotely resembles a political stance. And, if you're not outraged about any or all of the above, there's an outrage for that, too. There's even a term for the exhaustion caused by ongoing outrage: exhaustion fatigue.

Because of all this collective fury, I'd like to put forward a controversial idea (no, I'm not talking about an all-emoji newspaper again): the interrobang.

The interrobang (‽) is the passionate love child of the question mark and the exclamation point. And, while it is currently considered a nonstandard form of punctuation, it simultaneously questions your competence and yells at you.

How dare you take _____ position on _____ issue‽

Who do you think you are‽

You put pineapples on your pizza‽

What's wrong with you‽

The interrobang is distinctly American: insulting, yet efficient. And I think it fits our time perfectly.

Conceived by Martin Speckter in 1962, the interrobang actually gained some popularity for a hot second. And, although most of our current computer fonts don't support it, the interrobang was available on select typewriters in the late 1960s into the 1970s. And, while you will find the word "interrobang" in the dictionary, you won't find the symbol on your keyboard.

I think we're living in the midst of the interrobang era; therefore, it's time to bring it into the mainstream. But in order to type it easily, we'd have to vote off one of the characters on our standard computer keyboards. What symbol gets the boot? How about the tilde (~)? Or maybe the little upside down v caret thing above the 6 (^)? When's the last time you used either of those? Probably never.

In the same way that the Merriam-Webster dictionary adds words based on popular usage (and not necessarily critical approval), what does it take to get a punctuation mark added to common usage? If *listicle* and *humblebrag* made their way into the dictionary last year, the interrobang should receive serious consideration as an addition to our bag of punctuation options.

Extroduction

If *prelude* and *postlude* are each other's yin and yang, respectively, why not pair *introduction* with *extroduction*? Let's make "extroduction" a thing. I'm talking to you, dictionary people!

All joking aside, having a basic grasp of good grammar is a genuinely viable way to get a leg up these days, whether you're looking for friends, a good job or a long-term romantic relationship. If you find my stats and stories intriguing and/or valuable, do me a favor: look up your high school English teachers on Facebook and send them nice notes. Even better, get their addresses and mail them a holiday card with a photo of you wearing a festive sweater on it. Just make sure not to put an apostrophe in your family's last name; your teacher will be likely to mark it out with a red pen and mail it back to you.

We can become successful grammar citizens of the world without being mean about it. There is enough good grammar to go around. Don't treat your grammar righteousness like a blunt object against some poor soul who splits his infinitives. Perhaps there's a larger life lesson to be learned here, but I just hit my word count goal with this book, so it's going to have to be one of those things you figure out on your own. Thanks for reading.

Acknowledgments

Here's an incomplete list of fantastic people who helped this book become a reality.

First, I have to thank my wife, Carrie, for encouraging me to pursue my writing goals. You are literally the best.

To all the word nerds and grammar geeks who got really excited about this book and helped get the word out about it—thanks. Make sure you get your sticker.

Thank you to Dr. Elizabeth Ballard (a.k.a. Doc) for editing this mighty, mighty boss tome. Of all the books, this one will be scrutinized doubly for grammar mistakes! Your red pen is mightier, indeed.

Patrick Laurent of Laurent Collective (laurentcollective.com) made this book look legit. Let's be honest—we do judge books based on their covers. That's why I went to Patrick. Also, I feel fancy when I tell people that my book cover was created by my designer friend in London.

I want to thank my first editor, Sadie Hunter, and all the people at the *Current*, a publication which covers the Indianapolis north suburbs. Without you all there would be no "Grammar Guy." For the record, I wanted to be called "Word Nerd" or "Grammar Guru," but it's fine.

Thanks to all of the editors at the papers where Grammar Guy appears. Local newspapers play a crucial role in our society. Please support local journalism by purchasing a subscription. At the very least, click on all the ads on their websites when/if you read my columns online.

Everyone who gets a chance to visit the North Indy suburbs should spend some time and money at Noble Coffee & Tea in downtown Noblesville as well as Books & Brews (all locations, but especially the Noblesville location). While writing this book, I spent hours drinking various succulent liquids at these establishments.

Thank you to my friends at the National Society of Newspaper Columnists (columnists.com) and the Erma Bombeck Writers' Workshop (humorwriters.org) for embracing my quirky subject matter and making me feel like a "real" writer. When I spend time with you people, I feel as if I am spending time with family (at an old, haunted insane asylum).

Thanks to my launch team. You all helped iron out the kinks as well as get the word out about this book.

Notes

Second Introduction

Godwin's Law of Nazi Analogies:
Godwin, Mike. "Meme, Counter-meme." *Wired*, 10 January, 1994. Accessed at wired.com/1994/10/godwin-if-2

Social Success

Engfish:
Orwell, George. "Politics and the English Language." From *The Collected Essays, Journalism and Letters of George Orwell, Volume 4, 1945-1950*, edited by Sonia Orwell and Ian Angus. New York: Harcourt, Brace, Jovanovich, 1971.

Anagrams:
"What is the history of anagrams?" by Anagrammy Awards. 10 May, 2016. Accessed at anagrammy.com/articles/history.html

"Thomas Billon" from Wikipedia. wikipedia.org/wiki/Thomas_Billon

Mondegreens:
Sylvia Wright. "The death of Lady Mondegreen." *Harper's Magazine*, November 1954. Accessed at harpers.org/archive/1954/11/the-death-of-lady-mondegreen.

Conspiracy theories:
Bensley, D. Alan et. al. "The generality of belief in unsubstantiated claims." *Applied Cognitive Psychology*, 7 June 2019.

Interlude: Have the best words.

Funniest words:
Engelthaler, T. & Hills, T.T. *Behavior Research Methods*, 14 July 2017. https://doi.org/10.3758/s13428-017-0930-6

Batman quote:
Warner Bros. Pictures presents in association with Legendary Pictures, a Syncopy production, a film by Christopher Nolan; produced by Emma Thomas, Charles Roven, Larry Franco; story by David S. Goyer; screenplay by Christopher Nolan and David S. Goyer; directed by Christopher Nolan. *Batman Begins.* Burbank, CA :Warner Home Video, 2005.

Cellar door:
Barret, Grant. "Cellar Door." *New York Times Magazine*, 11 February 2010.

Crush it at Work

Correlation between good grammar and career success:
Hoover, Brad. "Good Grammar Should Be Everyone's Business." *Harvard Business Review*, 4 March 2013.

Scholars debate which words Shakespeare invented:
Scarborough King, Rachael. "Coined by Shakespeare? Think again. *Boston Globe*, 18 August 2013.

Action words aren't enough:
Cendella, Marc. "These are the 25 magic resume words that will land you the job: Ladders 2018 Resume Guide." From theladders.com, 26 January 2018. Accessed at theladders.com/career-advice/these-are-the-magic-resume-words-that-will-land-you-that-job-ladders-2018-resume-guide.

Exclamation points:
Eveleth, Rose. "The History of the Exclamation Point." Smithsonian Magazine, 9 August 2012. Accessed at smithsonianmag.com/smart-news/the-history-of-the-exclamation-tion-point-16445416/

Plenty of Fish Conversation Nation Study 2018. Accessed at drive.google.com/file/d/11uufDmFJc6Duq9_zrQuJzfXMpAuKIQwg/view

Steve Jobs' first online pizza order on CyberSlice:
"The NeXT Generation: How Steve Jobs Changed the Way We Sell Pizza." *PMQ Pizza Magazine,* June 2019. Accessed at pmq.com/the-next-generation-how-steve-jobs-changed-the-way-we-sell-pizza/

Kelsey Grammer:
"Kelsey Grammer." IMDb.com. Accessed at imdb.com/name/nm0001288/

Win at Life

NFL fans and spelling:
Foster, Geoff. "Washington Redskins: Bad at Football, Worse at Spelling." *The Wall Street Journal,* 28 April 2015. Accessed at wsj.com/articles/washington-redskins-bad-at-football-worse-at-spelling-1430252386

Adulting:
Fry, Richard. "It's becoming more common for young adults to live at home – and for longer stretches." Pew Research Center, 5 May 2017. Accessed at pewresearch.org/fact-tank/2017/05/05/its-becoming-more-common-for-young-adults-to-live-at-home-and-for-longer-stretches

Tater tots:
Billotto, Heidi. "Culinary Corner: The Fries Have It." WSCO-TV Charlotte, 6 June 2007. Accessed using the Internet Archive Wayback Machine at web.archive.org/web/20090403031908/http:/www.wsoctv.com/food/13455388/detail.html

Weight of the Eiffel Tower:
"The Eiffel Tower at a Glance." Accessed at toureiffel.paris/en/the-monument/key-figures

Invention of tater tots:
"Ore-Ida Fun Zone - Fun Facts." Accessed using the Internet Archive Wayback Machine at web.archive.org/web/20060622162414/http:/www.oreida.com/funzone/funfacts.aspx

The Latinists:
Salmon, Vivian. The Study of Language in 17th-Century England: Second Edition. John Benjamins Publishing Company, 1988.

Blame Noah Webster:
Scudder, Horace E. *Noah Webster.* The Riverside Press, Cambridge, 1890.

Evel Knievel:
Dostis, Melanie. "Looking back on Evel Knievel's most memorable jumps on his birthday." *New York Daily News,* 17 October 2015. Accessed at nydailynews.com/entertainment/back-9-evel-knievel-memorable-jumps-article-1.2400785

Mettle:
From *Merriam-Webster Dictionary.* Accessed at merriam-webster.com/dictionary/mettle

Eggcorns:
Lieberman, Mark. "Egg Corns: Folk Etymology, Malapropism, Mondegreen, ???" *Language Log,* 23 September, 2003. Accessed at itre.cis.upenn.edu/~myl/languagelog/archives/000018.html

Lucky in Love

Dating studies:
Biziorek, Travis. "How Good Grammar Increases Your Chance for Finding Love." 4 February 2013. Accessed at kibin.com/essay-writing-blog/grammar-gets-love

Murray, Megan. "How Your Geek Life Affects Your Love Life." 23 May 2018. Accessed atzoosk.com/date-mix/dating-data/geeks-in-love

Mager, Michael. "Could Bad Grammar Mean a Lonely Valentine's Day for Dating Hopefuls?" 1 February 2016. Accessed atgrammarly.com/blog/could-bad-grammar-mean-a-lonely-valentines-day-for-dating-hopefuls

Over vs. more than:
McIntyre, John. "Hey, Associated Press Stylebook, some friendly advice: 'over/more than.'" *The Baltimore Sun,* 31 October 2013. Accessed at baltimoresun.com/opinion/columnists/mcintyre/bal-hey-associated-press-stylebook-some-friendly-advice-over-more-than-20131031-story.html

Prefix *as-*
Accessed at dictionary.com/browse/as-

Valentine's Day:
Marr, Michael. "SOUL FOOD:Various versions of the origin of St. Valentine's Day." *Daily Pilot*, 8 February 2007. Accessed at latimes.com/socal/daily-pilot/news/tn-dpt-xpm-2007-02-08-hbi-soulfood08-story.html

Become King of the Word Nerds

Richest Americans:
Kroll, Luisa and Kerry A. Dolan. "Billionaires: The Richest People in the World." *Forbes*, 5 March 2019. Accessed at forbes.com/billionaires/#7773ed28251c

Correlation between introverts and good grammar:
Boland, Julie E. "If You're House Is Still Available, Send Me an Email: Personality Influences Reactions to Written Errors in Email Messages." PLoS ONE 11(3): e0149885.
Accessed at https://doi.org/10.1371/journal.pone.0149885

Underground supervolcano in Yellowstone Park:
Breining, Greg. *Super volcano: the ticking time bomb beneath Yellowstone National Park.* St. Paul: Voyageur Press, 2007.

Yoda:
Pereltsvaig, Asya. "On Statistical Universals." From Languages of the World, 17 May 2011. Accessed at languagesoftheworld.info/linguistic-typology/on-statistical-universals.html

Star Wars vs. Star Trek fans:
Hertzberg, Karen. "Star Wars vs. Star Trek: You Can't 'Force' Good Writing." From Grammarly, 4 May, 2016. Accessed at grammarly.com/blog/star-wars-vs-star-trek-you-cant-force-good-writing/

Interrobang:
Martin Spekter obituary: "Martin K. Speckter, 73, Creator of Interrobang." *The New York Times*, 16 February, 1988.

Index

CPSIA information can be obtained
at www.ICGtesting.com
Printed in the USA
LVHW091449120321
681182LV00007B/62